BEYOND WORDS
AND
THOUGHTS

Other Writings of Joel S. Goldsmith

Beyond Words
and
Thoughts

Joel S. Goldsmith

Edited By
Lorraine Sinkler

I-Level
Acropolis Books, Publisher
Lakewood, CO

BEYOND WORDS AND THOUGHTS
First Acropolis Books Edition 1998
© 1968 by Emma Goldsmith

All Bible quotations are taken from THE KING JAMES VERSION

Published by Acropolis Books, Publisher, under its *I*-Level imprint, under an arrangement with Citadel Press, an imprint of Carol Publishing Group.
All rights reserved.

Printed in the United States of America.

For information contact:

Acropolis Books, Inc.
Lakewood, Colorado

http://www.acropolisbooks.com

Library Of Congress Cataloging-in-Publication Data

Goldsmith, Joel S., 1892–1964.
  Beyond words and thoughts / Joel S. Goldsmith; edited by Lorraine Sinkler.
- - 1ˢᵗ Acropolis Books ed
      p.   cm.
  Includes bibliographical references.
  ISBN 1-889051-37-3 (hardcover : alk. paper)
  ISBN 1-889051-36-5 (paperback : alk. paper)
  1. Spiritual life.   I. Sinkler, Lorraine.   II. Title
BP610.G64145   1998
299' .93–dc21
                                                              98-42581
                                                                   CIP

This book is printed on acid free paper that meets the American National Standards Institute Z 39.48 Standard

Except the Lord build the house,
they labour in vain that build it. . . .
                                    –Psalm 127

"Illumination dissolves all material ties and binds men together with the golden chains of spiritual understanding; it acknowledges only the leadership of the Christ; it has no ritual or rule but the divine, impersonal universal Love; no other worship than the inner Flame that is ever lit at the shrine of Spirit. This union is the free state of spiritual brotherhood. The only restraint is the discipline of Soul; therefore, we know liberty without license; we are a united universe without physical limits, a divine service to God without ceremony or creed. The illumined walk without fear–by Grace."

                        –*The Infinite Way* by Joel S. Goldsmith

TABLE OF CONTENTS

TABLE OF CONTENTS

TABLE OF CONTENTS

THE WAY OF GRACE

Receptivity to God's Grace, Essential–Let the Divine Destiny Be Revealed in Us–God Translates Itself in Terms of Human Needs–God's Grace Is Not the Prerogative of One Sex–Prayer, an Opening of Consciousness–Teaching Givingness–God's Grace, the Gift of Himself–God's Grace Is Dependent on the Awareness of Our Relationship of Oneness with Him

BEYOND THE PAIRS OF OPPOSITES TO BEING

Grace Appears as Form–Goodness and Badness, Human Evaluations–Both Goodness and Badness Must Give Way to Being–Supply, an Activity of Consciousness, Not a Reward for Goodness–Become an Instrument as Which God Is Living on Earth–Living, Not Preaching, Attracts–Evil, Spiritual Ignorance–*I* Is the Word

INCORPOREALITY: GOD, MAN, AND UNIVERSE

Attain the Fabric, and the Form Follows–Incorporeal God Can Create Only Incorporeal Man–Evolving Stages of Consciousness–God Reveals Itself in a Moment of Unknowing–The Omnipresence of *I–I* Incarnate in Many Forms–*I* Speaks and *I* Hears–Because of Incorporeality, Givingness Results in Multiplication–In Healing, You Are Dealing with Incorporeal Man–Only Spiritual Discernment Can Reveal Incorporeality–Understanding Incorporeal Man Reveals the Essential Equality of Man–Mysticism Is a Rising into Incorporeality

TABLE OF CONTENTS

"HIS RAIN FALLS"
God Neither Punishes nor Rewards–As Ye Sow–Relying on Effect Is Sowing to the Flesh–To Be Born into an Unillumined Family Is to Be Born into Limitation– Recognizing the Invisible–Spiritual Ignorance Is the Barrier–Karmic Law on a National Level

GOD REVEALING HIMSELF AS CHRIST ON EARTH
Right Identification–God Revealing Himself on Earth– The Infinite Nature of Consciousness–The Indissoluble Union–The Tempter–The End of the Search– Infinite Individuality Fulfilled–Secrecy Imperative–*I*, Crying Out

Beyond Words
and
Thoughts

~ 1 ~

TOWARD THE EXPERIENCE

The heart and soul of the mystical life is an inner experience, and no matter what mode or method is used, that experience is possible if the basic motive is to discover truth. As long as you are just seeking to demonstrate health, supply, or companionship, however, there is no hope of attaining the God-experience. In spite of how successful you may be in human achievement, you will never attain spiritual awareness. That comes only when you have "died" to caring about the outer scene and are willing to take life as it is and work from within toward the goal of God-realization.

The Infinite Way came into being when I realized that there is no God in the human world. If there were a God in the human world, rape, arson, murder, wars, dens of iniquity, drug addiction, and all the other afflictions of mankind would be impossible. Not one of these evidences of man's inhumanity to man could occur in the presence of God. Everything that is taking place in this world of ours is taking place only because there is no God in the human scene.

This was the original unfoldment that was given to me some time after 1909, and this is what started me on the search. I have never doubted that there is a God, but now at least I know that there is no God in "this world,"[1] and I know now, too, that all the going to church and all the praying are not going to bring one here. People have been going to church to pray since before the days of the ancient Hebrews and have done so continuously ever since. They have prayed every kind of prayer that has ever been known, and still the world keeps right on falling apart.

Thus the search began: Where is God? What is God? How do we bring God into our experience? Eventually, late in 1928, the Experience took place, that first God-experience. This Experience brought with it no message, no words, no rules, nor were any principles given: there was just an experience that could not be described. Whereas in one moment I was like every other human being, in the next moment my body was well, and many undesirable human habits were gone. I found that a healing power was present and that I was on the threshold of a whole new life. The old life was dead; a new one had begun, but without a teaching, without any principles, without any laws—all this just because of an experience.

When you examine the lives of the mystics, you will find that that is what happened to them. Not one of them ever studied to become a mystic: each one had an experience, and that experience changed his life. As a matter of fact, in every case the mystic was able to give that experience to those who became his disciples and followers, and some of those in turn were able to give the experience to their disciples and followers. But with each generation, it became a less vital experience until finally it vanished almost completely.

The Importance of the Experience

The essence of living and healing through the Infinite Way is this experience. Those who have done healing work through the light given them in this message know that there is nothing in the teaching that heals. No matter what there is in the Infinite Way writings that you know and repeat, it will not heal you or anybody else of anything. You are not going to be able to heal until you have an experience, and with *every* healing there must be an experience until the time comes when you are so living in it that it may be necessary to renew it only once, twice, or three times a day, and then throughout the day all the other healings take place because you are living in that experience.

At first you may have to remind yourself: "I am not going to God to get any God-power. I am certainly not going to God to try to heal 'man, whose breath is in his nostrils.'[2] I am here only to realize the Christ, to feel the presence of the Christ. 'Speak, Lord; for thy servant heareth.'[3] "

You maintain a listening attitude until you feel some measure of release within, sometimes even receive a message, and then your part of the work is done. In some unknown way, the discords evaporate, harmony appears, and it would seem as if a bad person were changed into a good one, a sick person became well, or a poor person became more affluent.

But that is not it at all! What has really happened is that more of the spiritual nature of God has come into manifestation. Sometimes the healing is instantaneous; sometimes it takes place after the second or third realization; and sometimes you may have to work with a person for a year or two or three. That has to do with his receptivity, his ability to yield, and also with the heights that you attain.

Motive

You might rightly ask, "Then what is the good of all this teaching? What is the good of all the years of study of these books?" And I will say to you that the Experience will not come without that. The study, the practice, the listening, and the reading are the steps that break down the mortal sense into which we were born, that enable us to "die"[4] to mortal sense and to be "reborn."

Probably without the reading that I had been doing in the Bible and the Christian Science writings, and without all those years from 1909 until 1928 in which I was breaking my heart and head trying to find God, the Experience might not have come to me. In other words, every effort that I made from 1909 on to break through the darkness and to discover the secret was a helpful step leading me ultimately to the Experience.

That is why I have said in the Writings that it makes no difference what your background of study is if your primary object is to seek and discover truth. It would not make any difference if you were studying with the Hottentots or were with some other paganistic teaching as long as the motive behind your study was to seek the Experience, to seek the realization and the understanding of God. Ultimately, you would arrive, because different persons have been led to that point from many different directions—through paganistic teachings, through Christian teachings, or through non-Christian teachings—and they have attained, irrespective of their particular approach.

In the message of the Infinite Way, certain things have been revealed to me since my first experience that make it easier for anyone else with the right desire to attain it. Scripture says, "And this is life eternal, that they might know thee the only true God."[5] On that statement you can rest because that is the truth. If you can come to know God, you will attain the Experience: the God-experience, the Christ-experience, the spiritual Experience.

The first principle of the Infinite Way, therefore, is to know the nature of God, and that must be followed by an understanding of the nature of error and the nature of prayer. If you study every Infinite Way class that has ever been given, you will discover that not in any one of them have I ever omitted teaching the nature of God, the nature of error, and the nature of prayer because with this for a foundation, the Experience is not difficult to attain.

False Concepts of God

To begin with, the world believes, and most religions teach, that God is a great power and if only a person can get in touch with that God, It[*] will overcome his sins, diseases, lacks, limitations, and all his troubles. As long as you believe that, you are so far removed from ever attaining the Experience that you are hopelessly lost. The only possibility you would have of surmounting this obstacle is that your own basic search for God would in the end enable you to attain the Experience, not because of the teaching you are following, but in spite of it. The

---

[*] In the spiritual literature of the world, the varying concepts of God are indicated by the use of such words as "Father," "Mother," "Soul," "Spirit," "Principle," "Love," and "Life." Therefore, in this book the author has used the pronouns "He" and "It," or "Himself" and "Itself," interchangeably in referring to God.

more you seek to reach such a God, the further away God is. There is no God that overcomes the errors of the world. If there were, in all these thousands of years He would have been discovered, and the woes of the world would be at an end.

So you must begin with the realization that you are not going to God for a God-power: you are going to God to commune with Him, to tabernacle with Him, to experience, to feel, to speak to God, and to hear Him, but not for a power to do things for you. Any thought of power that enters your consciousness separates you from God.

All religions teach that God rewards and that God punishes, and as long as you are under that belief you cannot find harmony because you will be seeking to be good so that God will reward you and striving to give up all your errors so that God will not punish you. All such efforts only attest to the depth of your darkness. God has no interest in your goodness and will not reward it, and God has no interest in your sins and will not punish them.

Is there any reward for goodness? Is there any punishment for sin? Of course there is! But it is you who set in motion the rewards and the punishments—not, however, in the way that has been taught. What sets in motion the rewards and the punishments is the kind of sowing you do. If you sow to the Spirit, you set in motion your freedom and your release from "this world"; but if you sow to the flesh, you sow to corruption. Sowing to the Spirit means acknowledging Spirit as the source and cause of all that is, acknowledging Spirit as the activity of divine Grace, acknowledging Spirit as the presence, substance, power, law, and activity of Being.

That Something

"In all thy ways acknowledge him."[6] Acknowledge Spirit in all your ways; acknowledge that Spirit is the source of all. Then you will discover that it will not be very long until that acknowledgment dissolves your sins, false appetites, fears, doubts, geeds, lusts, and mad ambitions. The moment *you* try to dissolve these, you are in psychology, and psychology cannot succeed because it cannot make you other than you are.

Whatever your nature is, that is what you are going to remain until *something* enters your consciousness that brings about a change. It has to be something within yourself that transcends your little self and performs the healing, but that something will not happen while you are saying, "Oh, dear God, please save this person." Nothing of that nature will do it.

Whatever fruitage comes does not come because of all the statements that are in the books. If statements healed, then everyone who read those statements could go out and heal. The fruitage comes because the principles in those books, if they are studied and practiced and followed, will lead to the God-experience, and then when the Experience comes, it is this Experience that does the work.

Let the Mind Rest

You cannot reach God through your mind. It has been tried in every religious, philosophical, and metaphysical teaching in the world. Once you begin to perceive that truth, you will be halfway home. You must bring your mind to a place of stillness where the mind is transcended and your Soul-faculty receives the Experience. Everyone in the world has a Soul-faculty because God incorporated in us the nature of His own being, and therefore we have that within us which enables us to know God aright.

The people whose experiences are recounted in the Bible did not know the difference between Soul and mind; they did not know the difference between Spirit and the intellect, except for a few. One of those few was Paul, who said, "For the letter killeth, but the Spirit giveth life."[7]

The mystic who wrote *The Cloud of Unknowing*[8] knew that you must have discernment, not knowledge. He knew that no one can ever reach God through knowledge. God can be attained only when that altitude of consciousness which this mystic described as "unknowing" is reached, and that "unknowing" does not mean ignorance. It means a state of consciousness where the mind is at rest and the Soul-faculty can receive the things of God.

"The natural man receiveth not the things of the Spirit of God."[9] The "natural man" who is carnally minded "is not subject to the law of God,"[10] and the "natural man" functions through his mind. Only through his mind! How else can the "natural man" function? Even the things he does with his body are done because he is functioning through his mind. He cannot live without his mind; he cannot move his body without his mind; he cannot love without his mind. Nothing can a man do in this world without his mind, *but with his mind he cannot reach God!*

If you have caught some glimpse of the nature of God, you will know enough to stop trying to reach God, and you will relax and let God reach you. "The Son of man cometh at an hour when ye think not."[11] In the moment that you are not thinking, that you are at rest—not when your mind is dead, not when it is unconscious, but when you are not thinking and you are receptive and responsive—your Soul-faculty unites with God. That is the union which has been called the marriage with God. It is that moment when you are so still that the Soul of you, which is the individualization of God, comes into awakening—not that It awakens. No, no, no! It does not awaken. You awaken to It. The Spirit of God in you is in full bloom all the time. It appears to awaken, but it is you who are awakening to It—but not through the mind!

Surrender Yourself to God

If you are looking up to God, wanting God to do something, and trying to get God to come down to you, you are "out to lunch," just not around where God is. You must become convinced that God does not reward good and God does not punish evil. Whatever reward or punishment comes is from within your own self as is evident from all the good people in the world who are suffering and all the bad people who are prospering.

You must understand that the nature of God is not a power that will fix everything that is wrong in the world. It is power in the sense that it maintains order and balance in the universe, but it is not power in the sense that it will do something to evil.

Furthermore, God is not something that can be used. Man has always tried to make of God a servant: "Dear God, take care of my rent next month"; "Dear God, make my digestive apparatus work"; "Dear God, protect my child." God is thought of as a servant doing man's will. But there is no such God! You cannot make God do your will. You cannot influence God: not by praying, not by being good, not by fasting, not by tithing. You cannot influence God, and unless you can see that, you are not coming anywhere near the Experience. Once, however, you have come to the realization, "I cannot influence God; I cannot get God to do my will," you can settle down in peace and quiet and say, "Well, God, maybe you can influence me." That would be a twist!

Then you will understand what the mystics mean when they write that you must surrender yourself to God, that you must yield yourself to God, and why Jesus could say, "Nevertheless not my will, but thine, be done."[12] It is foolish to have a will of your own, even a will to see your friends healed, even a will to see peace on earth. Do not have any will at all, but retire within as many times a day as you can find a minute to remember, "Nevertheless, Father, not my will, but Thine be done on earth as it is in heaven." Relax and rest, and be a beholder of what God's will is. It might even include peace on earth if only you could let that will of God come through, instead of treating Him as if He were some kind of a servant that you were going to direct.

The Universal and Impersonal Nature of God's Activity

Do you see why the God-experience can come only when you have relaxed your personal efforts, when you have quieted your mind, when you have come to the realization that there is nothing personal about the activity of God in the sense that God would do any more for me than He would do for you? Never believe that God did more for Jesus Christ than He would do for you or for me. There is no such God!

God is not a superperson who goes around saying, "I will do this for this you here, but I will not do it for that you over there," or "I will do this for my good Hebrew people, but I will not do it for you Christian people." Is that not nonsense? God must be understood as universal Being. There are no exceptions in the laws of God. It can make no difference to God whether a person is white or black, Jew or Gentile, bond or free, saint or sinner. It can make no difference whatsoever!

Let the sinner but open his consciousness, and God will come to him just as quickly as He will to a saint. The Master even went so far as to say that God has more pleasure in one sinner that is redeemed than in ninety-nine[13] who think they are already good. Even that is not so: it is not that God has more regard for one sinner or more pleasure in one sinner redeemed. No, God is too pure to behold iniquity, and God has no knowledge of any sin or of any sinner.

The activity of God is like light touching darkness. It does not do anything whatsoever to darkness: it does not heal it, correct it, change it, or remove it. It just reveals that there is none. That is what the activity of God is like. In healing, It does not heal a disease: It just reveals that there is none. It does not reform a sinner: It reveals God's man, who never sinned.

There is that part of us which has never sinned, never been sick, was never born, and will never die, and the activity of God is to reveal that man. To our sense, that may remove sin, disease, or lack, but that is only to our limited sense. It does not really do it any more than light removes darkness. What light does is to reveal the absence of darkness, the nonentity of darkness, the nonexistence of darkness.

So it is that what we call a human being, "the natural man," has an existence only in the universal mind which is separate and apart from God. The whole of the human experience is an imaginary experience, a dream-experience, taking place in the universal mind which does not have its seat in God. The proof of that is that in the moment that you can still that mind and open the door for the Spirit of God to come in, that man is not there any more. That man of sin, disease, and death is just as absent as is the darkness when light touches it. We say that the "old man"[14] has "died" and the "new man"[14] has been "reborn," but where did the "old man" go? He did not go any place: he was not there to begin with!

Error, a Mind-formation

You will discover that almost as much attention is given in the Infinite Way writings to the nature of error as to the nature of God. The world believes that it knows what error is. To the world, it is a terrible and great power: it has the world in its grip, producing juvenile delinquency, gambling, drug addiction, rape, arson, murder, and wars. Everybody knows what evil is. If only someone could get God to do something about it! But in this message it is clearly revealed that you do not have to get God to do anything at all about it because the nature of evil is the "arm of flesh,"[15] or nothingness.

"Resist not evil"[16] is the Master's teaching, and that is the mystery of the healing ministry. When, in your healing work, you can sit down with the mind at rest and not battle the appearance, not fight it, not try to remove germs from someone's body, not try to dissolve lumps and reduce fevers, not try to heal insanity, but rest in that inner peace and quiet and assurance that there is only one law, spiritual law, and that all else is an image in the mind, the experience of God can take over, and then the healing takes place.

Has there ever been any more potent material law than that sitting in a draft or getting wet feet would give a person a cold? Now *materia medica* has discovered that it never was a law, that it was a superstition, an old wives' tale. Ah, yes, but many a cold has come about that way! But it was not from the wet feet or the draft: it was because a person accepted the universal belief that that would give him a cold, and it did. Now when it is known that it is not a law but a fairy tale, it is not feared.

Why should *materia medica* not eventually come to the realization that germs do not cause disease, but that germs are very natural, normal things? If God created all that is created, maybe He created germs, too. Metaphysical movements have been proving for the last ninety years that germ-diseases can be healed without antibiotics. All kinds of flu have been healed without medication of any kind.

If germs were destructive powers causing disease, do you believe that even one case could have been healed? If there has ever been a case of tuberculosis healed spiritually, then germs are not the cause of tuberculosis. If there has ever been a case of pneumonia healed spiritually, then the whole germ theory is wrong because none of the anti-germs has been used for the healing, nor has a power over germs or fevers been exercised. If germs caused fevers, they would not have been healed in every one of the metaphysical movements by persons who really had experienced God.

Merely stating that error is not power or that germs do not have power will not heal anything, but if you will work with that principle until the realization comes that germs have no power if Spirit is, if God is, you will bring forth healing. Many persons who are very good students of truth cannot heal because as long as they have only the letter of truth, they are believing it merely with the mind, and since it is the mind that has caused the difficulty, the mind is not going to cure it. The beliefs in the mind cause all the errors; therefore, another belief in the mind is not going to cure them. You must transcend the mind, and when you have transcended the mind all these things that the mind declares or believes in are proved unreal.

Humility

Work earnestly with everything you can find in the Writings about the nature of God and the nature of error because you will then begin to understand the nature of prayer. Once you understand the nature of God, you stop trying to reach out to God with your mind. It keeps you from praying the traditional prayer of begging and beseeching God, and makes you laugh at yourself to think that God is here to do your will or that you can influence God to do something that God is not already doing. All this begins to change your attitude and enables you to settle down into an atmosphere of receptivity.

Prayer is then no longer words or thoughts; prayer is no longer asking God to do something or expecting something of God: prayer now has a whole new meaning. It is a state of silence in which you become receptive to the word of God. The mind is still; the spiritual faculty is alert; and in the silence the grace of God is received. This is prayer.

Prayer has nothing to do with getting God to do something; prayer has nothing to do with getting God's power to destroy something; prayer has nothing to do with influencing God. God forbid that prayer should be used to tell God what to do, to influence God, or to bribe Him! Prayer is a state of silence in which you commune with God and receive His grace, where every Word that proceeds out of the mouth of God becomes power, and you become the receptivity through which It flows.

That is why the Master recognized that he was a servant, and in our relationship with God that is all you and I are. We are servants here, receiving the grace of God and allowing It to flow. Anybody who gets egotistical about that is going to lose his head because the closer one is to being a master, the more of a servant he will become and the more he will realize, "It is not I, of my own self, who am doing this. No, it is the flow that is taking place through me." There is your true sense of humility.

Humility does not mean being less than somebody else; it does not mean being less than anybody on the face of the earth. It means that as an avenue of God you are nothing but an avenue. Never will you believe that you have power to heal if you really understand the principles of the Infinite Way. Never will you believe that you have power to reform anybody or to give him illumination. No, you will understand yourself to be the instrument of God's grace, and the benefit that you can be to anyone is in proportion to your receptivity, your devotion, and your sacrifice of self.

It is the mind that parades and vaunts itself. Let the mind be still, and "at an hour when ye think not," behold the Experience.

~2~

BUILDING A CONSCIOUSNESS OF GRACE

It is not possible to reach God or to embrace truth through the human mind, although it is possible for truth to impart itself to us. It is unlikely, however, that the fullness of truth will be revealed to any one of us because, as human beings, we do not have the capacity to receive truth in its fullness. Instead, we receive certain facets, realizations, and principles of truth, which are continually flowing in proportion to our receptivity and openness.

Nothing that can be known with the mind is absolute truth; and therefore, we cannot depend on any statement of truth we know. In any and every experience, we must open our consciousness and be receptive to whatever may be imparted to us.

For this reason, we can never live on yesterday's manna, nor depend on anything we knew yesterday. In other words, if we are in meditation, we are not in meditation for the purpose of remembering something we have read in books: we are in meditation for the purpose of receiving an impartation from the Father within. That impartation may come to us in the form of a passage we have heretofore known in Scripture or in spiritual writings; but when it comes in the silence of meditation, it comes to us as an impartation from the Spirit, not as an activity of memory.

A Knowledge of Truth Develops Consciousness

The activity of the human mind is not power in the sense of spiritual power, and not all the knowledge that can be embraced in the human mind—even all the knowledge of truth—is spiritual power. Knowledge of truth acts to remove from us our ignorance of the nature of Spirit and its activities and operations.

An example of this is that when we first come to the study of truth we believe that if we can just reach God, we are going to have the power that will destroy all earthly errors; but, as our understanding of the principles grows, this ignorance is chipped away, and we stop looking to God with the expectation that He will remove the evils of "this world."[1] Similarly, as we learn through reading, listening, and study that there is but one power, we stop trying to use that one power to do something to another power called evil, sin, disease, or death. With this knowledge of truth, we are given the Grace to cease the mental activity involved in attempting to get God to overcome our enemies, and we are thereby enabled to relax inwardly and await the realization of Grace, which is the nonpower.

These principles of truth that we learn through study and practice develop our consciousness to the place where we "resist not evil,"[2] where we can put up the "sword,"[3] where we can retire within ourselves in an inner peace, and in that descent of peace become aware of Grace. That Grace is not a power: It is a presence, and in the presence of Grace there is no need for any power because nothing of an erroneous nature is there.

The Scriptural statement, "In thy presence is fulness of joy,"[4] is a clear promise that in God's presence there is no sin, disease, death, lack, or limitation because otherwise there could be no fullness of joy. So, in "thy presence," evil of any name or nature cannot function, for it has no existence. The study in which we engage leads us to a place in consciousness where we can relax, rest in a state of receptivity, and then eventually hear or feel something that would indicate, "Fear not, it is *I*.* 'It is I; be not afraid.'[5] Nothing shall in any wise come nigh thy dwelling place."

This must inevitably bring us to a place of resting from taking thought, realizing, "I cannot use Truth, but if I relax, Truth can use me, and It can function in my life. 'I live; yet not I, but Christ liveth in me.'[6] " But, if Christ is living our life, if Christ is functioning through us and as us, we are not taking thought or doing, and it is as if we were standing to one side, being a beholder of Christ, Truth, living our life.

As you are reading this, at the same time, be relaxing: let go of any and every thought. Release the belief that there is anything that you can do about anything. Relax; be still. Be still and *let* God be God. Recognize that you could not possibly embrace God in your mind. Let your remembrance be: "Christ liveth my life. God functions as my being." Let the whole earth be still, and above all let your mind be still.

As you relax in this surrender, letting the mind that was in Christ Jesus be your mind, Grace will begin to function. Grace will function as wisdom; Grace will function as harmony and peace; Grace will function as health, wholeness, completeness, inspiration, and as the source of all knowledge, and It will flow through you, in you, and as you.

---

*The word "I," italicized, refers to God.

Those who have been working with Infinite Way principles are now approaching the state and stage of consciousness that lives by Grace—not by physical might, not by mental power, not by knowledge, but by Grace. The knowledge of truth always serves a function in your experience in that such knowledge helps you to settle back into an attitude of expectancy. That is the only purpose that a knowledge of truth is serving at this stage of your unfoldment because now you should be rising above the letter of truth into the Spirit, into that area of consciousness where you live without words and without thoughts, above the law.

Grace, a State of Nonpower

There are physical laws that operate on the physical plane and mental laws that operate on the mental plane, and in your humanhood you live by these laws. In your spiritual attainment, however, at first you live less by physical laws and more by mental laws, and then eventually less and less by mental laws and more and more through Grace without any physical or mental laws operating because Grace transcends all law.

For example, the law of self-preservation keeps birds as far away from human beings as possible, and it is not often that you find birds making friends of human beings. Yet, there is the example of St. Francis, who proved that even this law can be transcended and that it is possible to live in such an atmosphere of Grace that birds will come to you and rest on your shoulders, your head, or on your hands.

Certainly, for the most part, human beings want to stay as far away from wild beasts as they can, yet there have been states of Grace where wild beasts could be faced without fear. Daniel demonstrated this, and many today have been able to prove that wild beasts do not always act like wild beasts. This would be true, however, only where an individual is living above the law and is under Grace, that Grace which is the absence of any power.

Once you realize that you cannot use spiritual power and you no longer rely on physical or mental powers, you then reach that attitude and altitude of consciousness which is a state of Grace, a state of nonpower, and you discover that what heretofore has operated as power is no longer power in your individual experience. That it will probably be a long time before the Grace-consciousness is demonstrated in its fullest degree is evidenced by the fact that after the Master's resurrection he was still full of nail wounds and knife wounds. To that degree, he was still under physical law.

The point is not whether you can, at this moment, walk on the water; the point is not whether you can deliberately swallow a bottle of poison and survive. That is not the point. The point is that from the moment you begin to function under Grace, physical and mental laws have less and less power over you. When you function under Grace, you may be called to those who have swallowed poison or to those who have been seriously injured, and by your realization of nonpower, you can bring them through it and lift them above whatever law they may have come under.

You must remember that to some extent, almost from the beginning of your experience in the Infinite Way, you have been under Grace. Every healing that you have witnessed has been a proof of Grace because the law involved has been overcome. If you have had a spiritual healing of a cold, the flu, pneumonia, or any of the diseases that are presumably caused by germs, it was Grace that proved that the material law was of non-effect. The law of germs, infection, or contagion could not operate where the consciousness of Grace is.

So it is that any healing—physical, mental, moral, or financial—is a proof that material law cannot function in the presence of spiritual consciousness. It is not that your developed consciousness of truth is a power over the law: it is a proof that the law is not a power in the presence of your consciousness of Grace.

The Reborn Consciousness

What constitutes your consciousness of Grace and how is it developed? It can be attained only by working consciously and conscientiously with the principle of one power, reading about it on every page of the Infinite Way books, and hearing about it on every Infinite Way tape recording. Through that, gradually your consciousness comes to accept the truth that there is but one power, and it is spiritual; there is but one law, and it is spiritual law. As your consciousness accepts this truth, material or mental law hits up against that developed consciousness, and like darkness, it is not there any more. That is how spiritual consciousness operates.

At first, spiritual consciousness is formed by an intellectual awareness of these principles. You come to accept God as your consciousness, as the only power. Over and over again the Infinite Way books hammer away at the theme that God is individual consciousness, your consciousness and mine. If God is your consciousness, what chance would anything have of operating for evil in that consciousness? Nothing shall "enter . . . that defileth . . . or maketh a lie."[7] Enter what? Enter God-consciousness, enter your consciousness because your consciousness is God-consciousness.

As you work with the Writings and are filled with the principle that God constitutes your consciousness and that your consciousness is the one and only power, you are building a consciousness of Grace. There is no power external to you. All power functions from within you, and it is only of a spiritual nature; therefore, it does not govern anyone, control anyone, or dominate anyone, but is a spiritual law of freedom unto everyone.

Then, lo and behold, when something claiming to be a law comes to your attention—something of your own, of your family, your patient, or your student—and it touches your consciousness, which is no longer your consciousness, but God-consciousness functioning as your consciousness, the one and the only power, and therefore the light of the world, what happens? Exactly what happens to darkness when the light shines. It disappears! You have not used a power; you have not even used the power of Truth: *you have been the power of Truth.* You have not used It: if anything, It has used you.

As you continue to abide in the principles that have been given to you in this Message, every principle that becomes a part of your consciousness constitutes the reborn consciousness, and the "old man,"[8] or the old consciousness that believed in or feared two powers, that used one power over another power, is "dying." The old consciousness is being educated out of itself. As this "old man" with his belief in two powers and his subservience to the law "dies," this new consciousness is born, and eventually you rise above the law into a consciousness of Grace in which you are not thinking in terms of overcoming or of power. You are not thinking in terms of words or thoughts: you are living; you are being; and you are letting the divine Consciousness flow through you, animate, and live your life for you.

The Grace-consciousness Lives as a Beholder

As a way station to this consciousness, you have had the Ten Commandments to tell you what to do and what not to do, and up to a certain extent you must have succeeded in attaining at least a goodly measure of obedience to them. Then, with the Sermon on the Mount, you went a step further. But in all of this, you were still living your life: you were trying to love your neighbor as yourself; you were trying to be philanthropic; you were trying to forgive your enemies; you were trying to improve yourself. All this is commendable and highly desirable, but it is not the ultimate goal of spiritual living.

When the new consciousness is attained, you have risen above trying to do or to be something of yourself: you are living by Grace, and it is the grace of God that functions through you as benevolence, purity, kindliness, and integrity, and you are now enabled to say with the Master: " 'Why callest thou me good?" [9] Why callest thou me spiritual?"

It is a state of Grace that is functioning in your life. You have no power to be either good or bad; you have no power to be spiritual or unspiritual; you have no power to be charitable or uncharitable. Whatever it is that is functioning through you, that is what you must be, and it is not your little self being it.

Your personal sense of "I" has moved over to where it is now only a beholder of life. It is always beholding and marveling at what things the Father is doing, but it is not participating—just beholding, beholding, and beholding.

It beholds sometimes with sadness. Can you not hear the pathos and the sorrow of the Master, "O Jerusalem, . . . how often would I have gathered thy children together, even as a hen gathereth her chickens under her wings, and ye would not!"[10] And with that same poignancy, the beholder sees this world and mournfully cries out, "Oh, it would be so easy to have world peace; it would be so easy with all of God's wealth that is in this world to have abundance for everybody, but 'ye would not.' " So he stands by, praying that consciousness be opened to receive Grace, to rise above this law of power.

No Power Is Necessary in a State of Grace

It is that word "power" that is a stumbling block. Man is always seeking a power, a power to overcome something or destroy something; and therefore he is not living in the awareness of God, because in the realization of the presence of God there is no power needed to overcome, to destroy, or to do anything.

Some people act as if God-power were necessary to increase the supply of this world. The supply of this world—and I am speaking of material supply—is already infinite. There is already more of whatever is necessary for food, clothing, and housing than the entire world could consume, and these forms of good are being renewed faster than they are being used. There is no need to turn to God for greater supply: there is need only for us to be willing to share the supply we already have.

The world prays to God for peace. God has no peace to give! God is not withholding peace. God's peace is already established, but peace must be established in the consciousness of the individual. If you and I are not at peace with each other, God can do nothing about it: it lies within you and me to decide what it is that will establish peace.

Peace is a state of Grace, and it functions in that moment when you are demanding nothing of another, when you are realizing that God's grace is your sufficiency in all things and that there is a sufficiency of God's grace omnipresent to meet the need of this and of every moment. In that realization, you free every person, and he can feel that you have freed him. He is at peace with you because the only reason for a lack of peace is fear, the fear of what the other person may want of you. Individually and collectively, nationally and internationally, that is the one fear, and the only antidote is the realization:

*I have a hidden manna. I have a hidden source of supply that is not dependent on "man, whose breath is in his nostrils."[11] It is not dependent on anyone's good will.**

---

*The italicized portions of this book are spontaneous meditations which have come to the author during periods of uplifted consciousness and are not in any sense intended to be used as affirmations, denials, or formulas. They have been inserted in this book from time to time to serve as examples of the free flowing of the Spirit. As the reader practices the presence, he, too, in his exalted moments, will receive ever new and fresh inspiration as the outpouring of the Spirit.

New Light on Forgiveness

People are at war within their own families—not over money particularly or over land, but because there is nearly always something that one is demanding of another that is causing a breach. The healing can take place only in release, and you can release every person only when that state of Grace has come to you and you realize that you no longer need power. Your oneness with God is your assurance of omniscience, omnipotence, and omnipresence, and because of that you can release anybody and everybody.

This might be called forgiving, but it is a far better way of dealing with the whole subject of forgiveness than the traditional approach. To forgive is difficult because forgiveness has always implied the forgiving of an actual wrong done, which in some way one is supposed to forget. This is rather difficult to do. It is far easier to forgive if you can see that the reason that you think a wrong has been done to you is because you were expecting something from someone, and you had no right to expect anything from anybody. So in the beginning it was your fault; you brought it on yourself. You expected something of someone; therefore, that person did to you what you are having a hard time forgiving. If you had not expected anything of him, however, you would have nothing now to forgive, and you and he would be at peace.

Grace Brings Freedom from Karmic Law

So it is that under the law of self-preservation you can see how we injure one another, all because we are trying to protect ourselves, or to save ourselves at somebody else's expense. Also, you can see how we have been taught to consider certain things as law which were not law at all, and we then have come under the belief of that law. For example, the Hebrews once taught that the sins of the fathers would be visited on the children unto the third and fourth generations, yet later this law was rescinded by the Hebrews themselves.

The truth is that you are under the penalty of your own thoughts and deeds, and under no other penalty. No longer can the thoughts and deeds of another operate against you. Now you are released from the sins of your parents and your grandparents. Now you turn within and realize what Paul said, "For he that soweth to his flesh shall of the flesh reap corruption; but he that soweth to the Spirit shall of the Spirit reap life everlasting."[12] So it is *your* sowing that determines your life. You are not under the law of domination; you are not under the law of anyone else's mental powers, sins, or fears. You have the choice to live either under the law or under Grace.

Man is a prisoner of mind-created laws which sooner or later will be revealed as not being law at all. This may take centuries, but today we are becoming aware of the fact that material and mental laws are law only while they are accepted in mind as law, whether it is the law of heredity, the law of racial belief, or the law of karma.

If the law of as-ye-sow-so-shall-ye-reap, the karmic law, is valid, think what penalty the United States has stored up for itself because of its dropping of atomic bombs. Try to think what degree of karmic law it has brought itself under, and if you are the kind of American who approves of this type of wholesale slaughter, you also are under that law. But that is law only to those who accept it as law, to those who accept the fanatical patriotism of "our country, right or wrong."[13] Actually, karmic law of any kind does not operate except for those who are prisoners of the mind and who, therefore, accept that law.

If you are abiding in Grace, there is no law. The law is the law to those who are still prisoners of the mind and live by it, but the law is not law to those who are abiding above the letter of truth, without words and without thoughts, above the law, abiding morning to night, night to morning in the realization:

"I and my Father are one."[14] *What can touch that oneness? Is there a law of matter or of mind that can touch God? If I and the Father are one, then I am that One, and that is the One who is not man, not a human being, but spiritual being.*

I am not man; I do not have to be forgiven. I and the Father are one, and that One is Spirit. That One is life eternal, the spiritual Self which I am.

You will not become that Christ-Self by reading books. The reading of the books will tell you of your *I Am-ness,* but then you must turn from the books to meditation and attain the realization of *I AM.* Your study of the letter of truth is primarily to lead you back into the kingdom of God within yourself where you tabernacle with your inner Self and receive therefrom the assurance, "Be not afraid, it is *I.* Thou art *I; I* am thou."

Then you are under Grace—not under the law, but under Grace—and there is no law touching the Grace that you are under that does not dissolve. You thereby arrive at a place above words and thoughts, above using any truth, to an abiding in stillness, in quietness, in peace, and if there are any words or thoughts to come, let them come from the divine Grace, from the Father within, from the *source*.

When the Master said, "I have overcome the world,"[15] did he not really mean that the law could not function? Did he not mean that he was living in a state of Grace where there are no laws? The law can operate only in the minds of those who are accepting law. "Know ye not, that to whom ye yield yourselves servants to obey, his servants ye are to whom ye obey?"[16] Will you yield yourself to the law or to Grace? Will you serve God or mammon? The question is whether you are letting the world of effect be the law unto you or whether you are living by Grace. Is money going to be your God? Is the law of health going to be your God? Is anything in the realm of effect going to be power? Or are you realizing that there are no powers?

Prisoners of the Mind

Through this, eventually you will be able to look down into the universal mind, which is the mind of mankind, and you will see how enslaved it is and how that entire slavery is within itself. For instance, one man may have to pass through a barroom, and he almost has to run through it, he is in such fear of those bottles there and of what is in them, a fear that he may pick one up and drink from it. Any power the bottle might have is in his mind: it is not in the bottle, because you and I can walk right through that same room, and we do not even see the bottles that are there because they are not in our minds as a power. You can observe what it is in this person's mind or that person's mind that is making him a prisoner of the mind, holding him in fear and in bondage to something that has only the substance of a mental image.

With another person, it may be gambling. He cannot rest while he has a dollar in his pocket. He must gamble it away! Why? The attraction is not out there at the gaming table, because it does not attract most of the people in the world: it attracts only the few who are prisoners of that particular form of bondage. Or it may be the person who gambles on the stock market on Wall Street. He is just as much a victim of gambling as the one at the ten-cent dice table, and if you could look into his mind, you would see what is animating him and pushing him. He is not aware of it: he is a victim of it.

You learn never to condemn, never, because the person who is afflicted with the two-dollar race track or the hundred-thousand-dollar Wall Street betting mania, the one with the alcohol or drug habit, or the sex problem is a victim. He is not a sinner: he is a victim; and he is a prisoner of his own mind. You can free him only when he is ready to be freed, when he appeals for help, when he asks for it; and you can free him only by being free yourself, recognizing Grace and not law. Then, you sit in a complete silence, without any thoughts.

Restoring the Mind to its Proper Function

Always remember in your treatment work not to be concerned if thoughts do not come. Do not be concerned if no truth comes to you. You are not the actor; you are not the healer; the concern is not yours. You are relaxing yourself into Grace, and Grace is going to do the work: you are merely going to be the instrument of Grace. Therefore, whether the problem is physical, mental, moral, financial, or one of human relationships, do not struggle to know any truth, do not strive to give advice. Be still! *I* within you am God, so just be still and let *I* be God, and relax in the Grace that realizes law is not power. The law of the mind is not power; the law of beliefs is not power. *Grace reveals nonpower!* The presence of Grace reveals the non-presence of power, of law.

So, as long as you can abide in an inner stillness, do not be concerned whether you have words or thoughts because it might well be that you have gone beyond that place of needing words and thoughts. Words and thoughts are part of the activity of the mind, and what we are trying to do is to rise above the activity of the mind into Grace.

In quietness and in stillness is the presence of Grace. In God's presence of stillness, quietness, and peace is fulfillment, divine harmony. You are at the place now of not overcoming, not destroying, not removing. All of us in the Infinite Way should move out of the state of mind that is overcoming, rising above, and destroying, into the realization of Grace which is the light that reveals no darkness. It does not remove it, it does not send it any place: it reveals its non-presence.

Do not try to do something to or for those who come to you with sin, disease, and lack. Be that state of Grace which reveals their non-presence! Where they went, or how, or when, you have no idea, and do not try because you will be trying to use your mind again.

Do not think for a minute that this will destroy your mind, because your mind will always have its function as an avenue of awareness. All that you are doing is stopping the false activity of making a power out of your mind, which it was never meant to be in the beginning. "Take no thought for your life, what ye shall eat, or what ye shall drink; nor yet for your body, what ye shall put on.[17] . . . The Son of man cometh at an hour when ye think not." [18] You are not to destroy your mind; you are not to give it up; you are not to surrender it: you are to allow it to settle into its normal function as an avenue of awareness.

Truth is infinite. How terrible it would be to try to grasp Truth! If the thought came to you, or if someone asked you, "What is Truth?" and if you could smile at the idea that anybody could know what Truth is and, like the Master, turn on your heel and walk away, think how much you would be proving. Who can know what Truth is? "I am . . . the truth."[19] Try to define what or who *I AM*. Impossible!

So, the closer you get to that place where your mind is not busy seeking for some truth, the sooner you will see that Truth keeps pouring Itself through you from the source—not a made-up truth, not a formula—Truth, not a truth that somebody wrote. But it is the truth that you know that helps build your consciousness to the point where you receive Truth Itself, and then the Grace which is your sufficiency is flowing in full measure.

~ 3 ~

"THOU SHALT NOT MAKE UNTO THEE ANY GRAVEN IMAGE"

The discords of this world arise because we have not consciously contacted the source of infinite good. We have lived and are living on knowledge gained through the mind which is limited to what we read, see, and hear. We are limited to our own strength and to our own talents, and in that state of separateness we have accepted the universal belief that self preservation is the first law of nature, which in the vernacular of today means, "Do others before they do you!"

If God is ever to function in your experience and thereby prevent the disasters of earth from touching you—the wars, famines, poverty, tyrannies, and injustices—it can come about only through making contact with the Father within to the point of realization. You have already discovered that all the words and thoughts you have been using have done little or nothing for you. You may have gone around hopefully repeating, "I am rich, I am rich, I am rich," and you were still poor; "I am healthy, I am healthy, I am healthy," and you were still sick; "I am spiritual, I am spiritual, I am spiritual," and you were still carnal. The reason is that none of these statements is truth. They are the truth about the Truth.

Words and Thoughts Are Not God

Thinking about God or repeating statements will not bring the experience of God. For example, you could think about music all your life and never be able to bring forth a single note. Thinking about music is not going to make you a musician. In some way or other, you must attain a consciousness of music.

So, also, the words you speak and the thoughts you think about God will remain purely a mental exercise and will not show forth in your daily life until you have experienced the Father within, until you have received from within your own being the assurance of His peace, His grace, His presence. When that assurance comes to you, it will be so sacred that you will not talk about it. You will share it only with those who show some desire to know God aright.

Over and over again, you will return to your inner communion, and one day it will dawn upon you that you never need go anywhere except within yourself, and when you go there you will find the Father there–perhaps not the first day, perhaps not the first month, perhaps not the first year. My own search took many, many years before the realization of this inner presence was attained. Who knows how long it will take for you to go beyond thinking thoughts about God to the Experience itself? We are all differently molded in consciousness.

There have been persons who have devoted their whole life to thinking about God; they have lived their whole life with a Bible in their hands; and they have not come within a billion miles of God. All they had were words in their minds, and those words are not and never will be God.

No words in the mind ever become God–not even the word God or the word Christ. I can tell you that God is not a word; Christ is not a word: God is an experience; Christ is an experience. You can experience God, and you can experience the Christ, but you can never know either God or the Christ with your mind. Since God cannot be known through the mind, thinking about God will not bring the knowledge of God.

If, as might sometimes happen, a figure appeared in your mind that looked like whatever it is you think Jesus should look like, that would not be the Christ. That would be an image in your mind, but unless this picture were merely emotionally induced it might indicate that you were experiencing a measure of the Christ. There is no doubt but that many persons induce pictures emotionally. There are persons in Europe who each year experience the nail marks of the Master in their body, and the world mistakenly looks upon them as mystics. In many cases they are emotional neurotics because all they do is live so in their minds with the mental picture of the Passion that eventually it externalizes itself. You could do the same thing if you wanted to spend enough years just dwelling emotionally on the Passion.

As a matter of fact, you can bring out anything you want on your body, if you determine to live inside long enough with the feeling of it. You can bring out an absolute purity, where not a suggestion of the impure ever enters your mind or body, if you want to devote enough time to attaining that. If you fill your mind with sensual thoughts, however, you can make your body so lewd that it would be a sin to turn it loose on the street. What you take into your mind with any degree of intensity must become manifest on the body because the mind and the body are one.

In the Third Dimension, Mind Is a Power

It is true that some very miraculous things have been done with the power of thought, and therefore misunderstanding sometimes arises about the function of the mind. The fact is that in the three-dimensional world mind is not only a great power, but it probably is a greater power than all the matter that could be assembled together. Mind can be used for constructively helping one's self and others, and mind can be used to destroy others, including the entire world and, in the end, destroying one's self with it.

There is power in the human mind on the three-dimensional level. If you were to hold on to good thoughts persistently—right thoughts, loving thoughts, and charitable thoughts—you would make some measure of progress in the direction of altering your nature and character. On the other hand, if you lent your mind to the obscene only, to the destructive and the carnal, there is no question but that in a few months you would tend to become that way and look like it, too, because whatever you are in your mind begins to show forth in your face.

In the third dimension of life, which is mind and matter, you have a choice. You can use the mind for good or you can use it for evil because the mind is but an instrument. It is never the mind that is the power: it is the individual on the human level who chooses whether he will use the mind for good or evil, and if he is using it for good, he will be sure that he is using it for impersonal good, not just for a particular person's good, which might be at someone else's expense.

In the Fourth Dimension, Mind and Body Become Instruments of Spirit

In the presence of the Spirit which is released when you touch the center of your being, neither matter nor mind can function in any injurious way in your experience. Matter and mind both become servants and tools, but never destructive ones. Your material sense of body becomes your instrument, to be governed and controlled by the Spirit within you.

Since you have a mind, naturally its function is to think, but it is not you who are thinking: it is the Spirit thinking, and then those thoughts are spiritual and eternal. Mind, thought, and body become instruments for the Spirit, and you become a blessing to this world. Your thoughts and your body are a blessing to all who come within range of you because all is governed by the Spirit which has been touched, consciously realized, and released in meditation.

Without this experience of meditation, you are living on words and thoughts, on that which is not the real power. It is only when the actual release of the Spirit in meditation comes that the great truth, "I live; yet not I"[1] is no longer a quotation: it is lived.

Religion Is an Experience

How many times have you heard the words, "Thy grace is my sufficiency in all things, and there is a sufficiency of Thy grace ever present with which to meet the need of this moment"? If you look out in the world, you know this statement is not true at all. As you look at the people who are sick, sinning, dying, in prison, and in every other kind of unhappy situation, your first thought is, "Why, that makes a lie out of this statement." Yes, but it was never meant that the words alone would meet your needs. It is God's grace that is your sufficiency: not the words. The words are only to tell you that if you attain His grace, the sufficiency is there.

The reason so many persons do not believe in the Bible is because they have read all the wonderful biblical promises, and it must be admitted that in the human scene there is no evidence that these promises are true. Hundreds of persons read, "God is our refuge and strength, a very present help in trouble,"[2] and forthwith they go out and get into trouble, and God is not there. Then they are tempted to think that the Bible lies.

The Bible does not lie. The trouble is that these persons have been depending on a quotation, not on God. They did not have God: they had a quotation, and they thought that the quotation was God. They thought that memorizing and reciting, "Neither shall any plague come nigh thy dwelling,"[3] was their protection. Then lo and behold, the next day when the plague did come nigh, they decided that the Bible was all wrong. But they had forgotten the first part of the Ninety-First Psalm: "He that dwelleth in the secret place of the most High shall abide under the shadow of the Almighty."[4] They forgot that the only one to whom the evils of this world do not come is "he that dwelleth in the secret place." For centuries, the Bible has been trying to reveal that religion is an experience, but the world has been living on a book full of promises instead of seeking the Experience.

Every day hundreds go to communion service, take a sip of wine, eat a piece of bread, and then think that they have communed with the Christ. Maybe up in their minds they have or in their imagination. But while the church service of communion is symbolic of true communion and is taken as if it were the real thing, it cannot be real because nobody can receive communion until he and the Christ meet within. True communion is an actual experience that takes place within when a person comes face to face with the Christ, when the Christ speaks or imparts Itself in some way or other. That is communion.

We have been led to believe that Jesus' crucifixion saves us from all punishment for our sins. According to that, when we are born, we should be provided with a certificate stating, "Sin all you like because Jesus was crucified, and we hereby give you a license to enjoy life." This is not true. And yet, symbolically, it is true because when the Christ is risen in you from the tomb where It is buried, your sins are forgiven you, and from then on, there are no more sins. The forgiveness of the Christ is always accompanied by the words, "Sin no more, lest a worse thing come unto thee."[5] You never quite forget that because it comes with a sharp voice. You say, "I thought You were so gentle." Yes, the Christ is gentle when the promise is, "Thy sins are forgiven,"[6] but the admonition that follows is a reminder to change your ways.

Everything in the Bible is truth when it is experienced. You can have Pharaoh at the back of your neck and the Red Sea in front of you, and you can come out without even "the smell of fire,"[7] if you have the Experience. That, however, does not mean just reading the Bible, quoting it, or memorizing it.

Anything and everything can happen to this world when it is living as a branch of a tree that is cut off. But life ceases to be a matter of chance after you begin the experience of surrendering your life to this inner Spirit, and then, under the guidance, direction, and protection of the Spirit, performing whatever you may be called upon to do in the outer world. There may be those who will be nurses, doctors, and lawyers, and those who will be mechanics, scientists, or teachers, but as long as the work is performed under the grace of God, it must be harmonious, successful, fruitful, and abundant, always with enough left over to share with those who have not yet awakened to the Experience.

The meaning of all true religion is the Experience. Whether in Buddhism you experience the Buddha or whether in Christianity you experience the Christ, it is the same thing. It means rising to the Fourth Dimension, to the consciousness of God.

Go Within

476

You may have known illness, lack, limitation, pain, accident, and unhappiness, because even though the relationship of oneness with the Father has always been the truth about you, you may not have had the consciousness of this oneness, you may not have had the inner assurance, nor had a contact with the source of your good.

But if it is really true that you and the Father are one and that the kingdom of God is within you, if you make this contact and receive an assurance from within, something that will let you feel, "Son, thou art ever with me,"[8] or "This is my beloved Son, in whom I am well pleased,"[9] or "My grace is sufficient for thee,"[10] you will then be able to prove that this Christ or Spirit of God lives within you.

Having the assurance of the divine Presence within you, you need nothing and nobody in this world. Once you have that awareness, you can go into the cage of a lion, even before its mealtime; you can travel the world without purse or scrip. If you have this assurance of Immanuel, what difference would it make if there were a Pharaoh breathing down the back of your neck and a Red Sea rolling up in front of you? What more would anyone need than to be walking around holding God's hand, feeling the Presence within, knowing that *"I* am with thee"?

You are not going to get this assurance from books, in holy temples, in fasting, or in feasting; you are not going to get it through rituals or sacraments. You are going to get it in one way only: searching for it and finding it where it is to be found—within you.

The only way in which you will attain positive proof that the kingdom of God is within you and will achieve the actual demonstration of oneness is by sitting alone, not making your needs known to the world at large, and turning within. In that period of aloneness, you may be borrowing the wisdom of Jesus, the wisdom of other mystics, or the teaching of the Infinite Way because probably up to this minute you have not proved that you and the Father are one. Now you must accept the truth and you must prove it:

I turn within: I am not turning up to the sky; I am not turning anywhere outside of my own being; I am not looking around for holy temples or holy teachers or holy books. I am turning within.

Here am I. The very seat and source of God is within me, the abiding place of God. God is within the inner sanctuary of my own being. I am not seeking for my life: what I shall eat or what I shall drink. I am not seeking for health, employment, or opportunities. I am seeking Thy kingdom, Thy grace.

Really, what I am seeking is the assurance that Thou art "closer . . . than breathing, and nearer than hands and feet,"[11] *that Thou knowest my need, and that it is Thy good pleasure to give me the Kingdom.*

So I am praying in secret. I am not letting any man know that I am praying. I am not letting any man know what things I have need of. I am not depending on "man, whose breath is in his nostrils."[12] *I turn within, and if this teaching is true, then God is right here, and I need go no further than right here where I am. I must know what it is that I am going for: for Thy grace, for the realization of Thy presence.*

In this meditation, I accept the truth that the place whereon I stand is holy ground because God is here. I accept God as omnipresence; I accept God as omniscience, the all-wisdom, knowing what things I have need of. I accept God as love, whose good pleasure it is to give me the Kingdom.

This Spirit which you have now contacted and with which you have become consciously one is the Presence that goes before you: your bread, wine, hidden manna, the meat the world knows not of.

The Miracle

This Presence, and not your mind or mine, is the healing agency. When anyone asks me for help, can you understand that the first thing that takes place in me is that my mind stops functioning, and I stop thinking? I think no thoughts of truth. I listen, and that lets the presence and power of God through to the patient;

whereas the moment I try to think a thought, even of truth, then I am trying to make thought a power; I am trying to make a statement of truth a power. No statement of truth is God-power; no thought of truth is God-power: only God is God-power.

So if you want God, be still; be still and let God function. Otherwise, you are letting your ego in, and what is worse, you are making graven images because whether you take a sentence and put it together and call it God-power or whether you take a wooden image and build it and make it God-power or you take a thought and make it God-power, what difference does it make? They are all graven images made by man.

The only thing that is not made by man is what functions through man in the silence. That he has nothing to do with. So when I am asked for help, immediately, no matter what I am doing, thought stops, and then whatever comes through, it is the presence and power of God that does the work. Sometimes I know what it is; sometimes it comes through in a message; but ninety-nine times out of a hundred I never know.

Many times students write to me and say, "Oh, this came to me, but I suppose you knew it in advance." No, I did not know it; I was not thinking of them; and I was not thinking of what message God was going to have for them. All I did was to be absent from the body, be absent from the mind, and let the Spirit perform Its function–not try to do it for the Spirit, not try to do it with the Spirit, but let the Spirit do it Itself, so that I did not have any graven images.

Any word of God that is in your mind is a word that you have created; it is a graven image. Any thought of God that is in your mind, you have created, and it is a graven image. If you want to be absent from the body, even the body of the mind, you must be absent from the body of thought, and then whatever God is, however God functions, something takes place in a way that seems to be a miracle to human sense. But it is not a miracle that has been performed: it is the presence of God realized.

No one understands better than I do the truth of the Master's statement, "If I bear witness of myself, my witness is not true"[13]–this power is not mine: this is God's. The more I can refrain from thought and be a receptivity, the greater presence and power comes through.

Surrender Your Mind to God

This truth can be taught only to those who understand that this is the "pearl of great price"[14] for which they are to sacrifice all. The principles of this work, as they are given in the Writings, must first be taught until there is a thorough groundwork in them. Then, when a student here or a student there with sufficient readiness is found, he can be carried one step, another step, and another, until you can say without shocking him and without making him think that God is a human being, "Stop looking for God. You have found Him; you are looking at Him."

Jesus could not tell everyone, "He that seeth me seeth him that sent me."[15] He could not! They would have said, "Why, that rabbi is going around saying he is God." Neither can you tell the person who has lived his entire life in the mind, in the intellect, "God is only present when all of that is given up."

But those who have come to the point of unfoldment where they are reading this book know that I am revealing to them the fruitage of practically forty years of spiritual searching. Such students are going to be far less concerned about an intellectual knowledge of God and the Infinite Way, and much more concerned with periods each day of experiencing God and gradually surrendering themselves unto God, while at the same time resting on the foundation of the letter of truth, the principles.

Everyone on this Path is really seeking to have God so govern his body that he will always be healthy, strong, and young, and with vital faculties. Everyone on this Path has to admit that that is his hope and his dream, but I am afraid that too few remember that this cannot be until they also surrender their minds to that same Spirit. They cannot have their minds run loose in one way and have their bodies governed in another way.

You receive the realization of God through the unconditioned mind, the mind that does not think personal thoughts, selfish thoughts, or evil thoughts, and in receiving the awareness of God in the mind, it becomes the harmony of the body, because mind is the substance of the body. Therefore, when the mind is full of God, the body is full of harmony.

"Thou wilt keep him in perfect peace, whose mind is stayed on thee.[16] . . . Lean not unto thine own understanding. In all thy ways acknowledge him, and he shall direct thy paths."[17] You must acknowledge Him in your mind as well as in your body, and if you want God-government of the body, you must accept God's government of the mind. When you go into meditation, you must be willing to receive God in your mind and not expect that God is going to do something to your concept of body without going through your mind. That just is not going to happen!

You have to surrender your business to God; you have to surrender your talent to God. You cannot have God's government in one part of your life and keep it out of another. I have had experiences in the past where I have been asked for treatment for a condition of health, and the person would say, "But do not treat me for smoking. I want to keep on smoking." If it is up to me to tell God what the person would like, I would be very glad to deliver a message. Whether He will perform it, of that I cannot be sure. He sometimes does not listen to me.

Complete surrender does not mean making yourself nothing, making yourself an automaton, or anything of that kind. It really means surrendering yourself to the influence of purity, harmony, and Grace in every area of life, and not saying, "I want to save out this part of my life for myself," because that is the barrier for many. They want a religious life, but then when they go to business, if they have to cheat a little or do a little false advertising, they do not want God to look in on that department. Actually, it does not work, and that is the reason for so much failure. We are holding out an area in which we really do not want God to interfere. "Give me health. Ah, yes, do that, but please let me alone over here. I am having a very, very good time."

The Impersonal Nature of God's Action

Since God does not function on a personal basis, God will not do anything for you personally. There must be within you always the remembrance that this that you seek, you seek for all mankind, for everyone, friend or enemy. It would be as impossible to channel God into you and your affairs as it would be to channel the rain into your garden. If you want to pray for rain, you had better pray for rain and not specify your or anyone else's garden. You will have to be willing for it to fall on the gardens of all those you do not like as well as those you do.

When you realize the divine Presence, you must include the prayer, "Let Thy grace be upon all mankind. Let all men be receptive to Thy presence." Whether or not they are is not the point. The point is that you are surrendering personal interest in the act of loving your neighbor as yourself.

There is no way to love your neighbor as yourself in a quotation. You can love your neighbor as yourself only in praying for yourself, and then including the neighbor—friendly neighbor, enemy neighbor—in the prayer. In other words, you have to realize the universal nature of God's grace and never believe that it can be channeled to good people only, or to white Anglo-Saxon Protestants. It does not function that way. God's grace is universal, and to love your neighbor as yourself means that when you do have this God-contact, you pray that it touches all mankind. Then you are surrendering all personal self-interest. You are praying aright.

Notice the emphasis on surrendering yourself to God, both mind and body. You are not choosing right thinking over wrong thinking, or pure thinking over impure thinking: you are opening yourself only to spiritual thinking, that is, to whatever flows forth from the Kingdom, the Consciousness within you.

When you go within, you are going within your own consciousness because that is where you live. That is the sanctuary of your being: your consciousness. As a matter of fact, it is not your consciousness, it is the divine Consciousness which you are. You are the divine Consciousness, and you go within to that Consciousness which you are, and out of the Consciousness which you are flows spiritual Grace.

~ 4 ~

Truth Unveiled

Every book of spiritual wisdom you have read has brought about a greater spiritualization of your consciousness, what might be called the peeling off of the onion skin, or the refining of consciousness. Each book, each class, and each principle taken into consciousness has prepared you for the one ahead, leading to greater unfoldment and toward that "act of Grace bestowed on individuals at a certain time in their unfoldment, lifting them into the master-state of consciousness."[1]

Always, since my first spiritual experience, living in two worlds has been difficult for me—living in that higher Consciousness and then coming down to earth, going back into that Consciousness and coming back down to earth—but never was it as difficult as in 1963. That year marked another period of initiation for me, but, even though in 1962 I knew it was to be, I had no knowledge of its intensity, its length, or the nature of the message that would be revealed.

It is not unnatural, therefore, that that year should have revealed the higher unfoldment, the higher Consciousness. This you will understand as you study the work that came through during this period. With each successive unfoldment, something was breaking through, leading to the teaching of going beyond words and thoughts, of going beyond the mind. This idea you will find in all the 1963 work,[2] revealing the nature of life as it is lived when you go beyond the mind and beyond thoughts: beyond taking thought, beyond reasoning. This is the revelation of the nature of Sabbath and of Grace.

A work of this kind leads to the highest point in consciousness that has yet been revealed in the Infinite Way, and it would seem that it is the high point in the revelation of both Moses and Jesus, and probably also that of Buddha.

The Middle Path

The fleshly sense of man cannot enter the kingdom of heaven, Spirit. The healthy fleshly sense is as illusory as the sickly sense, and the sense of good man is as illusory as the sense of bad man. The *middle path,* or spiritual consciousness, does not engage in exchanging the sense of erroneous man for the sense of correct man, but knows only spiritual man, or the son of God.

In healing work as understood in the Infinite Way, we are unseeing and unknowing the corporeal or physical sense of man: well or sick, rich or poor, good or bad. We are not unseeing or unknowing a corporeal man or a physical man for there is none, but we are unknowing or unseeing the corporeal or physical *sense* of man. The corporeal sense is the tempter. The healing truth is our consciousness of incorporeal man and the universe.

Melchizedek, or the Christ, who was never born and will never die, is the true man, and that which we see, hear, taste, touch, and smell is our false sense of that man. There is not a false man, a fallen man, or a physical man, but there is a false sense of man which we entertain.

The Meaning of Ascension

On the spiritual path, we begin our journey by studying the truth, learning and practicing the truth. We never attain the goal of realization, however, until we reach beyond the mind and its knowing of the truth to our becoming Truth: "That which I am seeking, I am!"[3]

On the Mount, in a high state of consciousness, Moses realized *I AM,* and thereby became *I AM.* Yet, there remained still a sense of Moses as is evidenced by the fact that he spoke of himself as being slow of speech. The realization of *I AM* prevailed, however, and with that great illumination came such a height of consciousness that he was able to lead the Hebrews out of slavery to the Promised Land. Had Moses been able to crucify or relinquish completely the mortal sense of himself which still remained, he would have been able to enter the Promised Land, or heaven. But he was bound by a finite sense of himself.

Jesus, however, not only knew the truth but *realized* and *became* the Truth: "I am the way, the truth, and the life."[4] Nevertheless, a sense of Jesus, the man, remained, because he said, "I can of mine own self do nothing. . . . If I bear witness of myself, my witness is not true."[5] This personal sense of self had to be crucified, as eventually it must be in all of us, or we will not ascend to the Promised Land, the realization of our spiritual identity.

Jesus' realization of the need to crucify, or rise above, the seeming mortal sense of self, enabled him to make the ascension. The ascension is always the same: a rising above mind, above knowing the truth, to Truth *Itself.*

In many classes and even in some of the Writings, I have said that I did not understand the reason for the crucifixion of Jesus: why it took place or why it had to take place if it had to. It puzzled me, and I have frankly admitted this. It was not until the year 1963, when I myself went through the experience, that the reason and need for the crucifixion of Christ Jesus was revealed to me. Somehow, after that experience, the memory of it passed from me, and I could not bring it to conscious recollection, until later the entire scene was revealed to me again when I went through the experience of ascension: that rising above mind to Truth Itself.

The Significance of Jesus' Experience on the Mount of Transfiguration

This is what I saw: In Jesus' statement, "He that seeth me seeth him that sent me,"[6] he revealed that he had attained the goal of *I AM*. " *'I am the way'*–thou seest me, thou seest God, for I and God are one." And there is an experience in which he proved this: he took three disciples to what is called the Mount of Transfiguration, which again is high consciousness, and he revealed to them the Hebrew prophets who were supposed to be dead.

But, to his enlightened sense, they were not dead, and he proved to his disciples that they were alive, and that they were with them there in form. Whether he translated them into visible form or whether he translated himself and the disciples into invisible form makes no difference because it is the same experience. He translated: he demonstrated to his disciples the truth he later proved: " 'I lay down my life, that I might take it again'[7]; *I* can walk into the invisible realm and *I* can walk out again, for *I* am Spirit, *I* am the way."

Because of Jesus' experience on the Mount of Trans-figuration, I understand now that crucifixion was not necessary for him, and that he could have avoided it. Enoch was translated without knowing death; Elijah was translated without knowing death; Isaiah, also, may have been translated. Therefore, it was shown to me through Jesus' experience on the Mount of Transfiguration that he could have been translated without knowing death, but when he became aware of the betrayal, the trial, and the threatened crucifixion, he chose to accept corporeal death in order to reveal to his disciples that death is not an experience, but an illusory sense that must be under-stood and seen through.

Death is not a condition that a person actually goes through. There is no death; no one has ever died. God has no pleasure in our dying. Death is an experience only of corporeal sense, the sense that testifies that we are physical, mortal, finite, but death itself is never an experience of our true being.

By permitting himself to experience corporeal death, Jesus revealed that there is no death, and he revealed himself in what appeared to be the same corporeal form with all its wounds. Then, having served this purpose, he had no other function here on earth. His continued presence would only have been an embarrassment to the disciples, to Rome, and probably to himself.

Jesus ascended out of corporeal form: he was trans-lated. This can be interpreted to mean that he rose beyond the mind; he rose above his own mind because it is only in the mind that the corporeal sense can be entertained, not in the spiritual faculties.

In our Soul-faculties, we are Spirit; we see each other spiritually, whether we are here on this plane, or whether we are looking at those who have gone to another plane, or to those who are not yet born.

Not Knowing the Truth, but Being the Truth

This revelation is the proof of the message that there must come a rest to *My** people. There must come a rest from the activity of the mind: taking thought for our life, fearing for our life, constantly knowing the truth in order to avoid some experience. There must come a Sabbath, and in this Sabbath we live by Grace, because then we do not know the truth, but Truth reveals Itself to us, and we become the Truth. It is not an activity of the mind: it is Soul revealing Itself.

When you reach that place where, instead of searching for a truth, feverishly reading or studying to latch on to some truth, you can relax and rest in the Truth—without taking thought, without speaking or thinking—you can be a state of awareness, and then you understand the meaning of "Man shall not live by bread alone, but by every word that proceedeth out of the mouth of God."[8] You will then discover that every word, every feeling, every emotion, and every thought that comes to you from the deep withinness of you is what you now live by. The Spirit within guides, It directs, It sustains, It protects, It goes before you to "make the crooked places straight."[9]

Our ultimate goal must be to live in, through, and as God. If we are not to do this, why did the Master teach, "Take no thought for your life"[10]? Life is meant to be lived by Grace, without might, without power. It is meant to be lived by every word of God that we receive

---

*The word "My," capitalized or italicized, refers to God.

in our consciousness. In the Infinite Way, students are being fed with the words of God that have been revealed by prophets, saints, and seers. These, the students take into their mind and bury deep in their consciousness until they, too, rise above the level of the mind to where they can live without taking thought.

Be receptive to the still small voice, for God is not in the whirlwind, God is not in your problems, God is not in your thinking, God is not in books: God is in the still small voice. How quietly and peacefully is it necessary to live within in order to hear that "voice," to receive Its impartations, and to partake of Its grace!

There is always a sufficiency of God's grace present for this moment, and therefore, we have only to be still in this moment in order to receive a sufficiency of Grace, but only for this moment.

The teaching of the Infinite Way is that the goal toward which we are working is the attainment of the realization that that which I am seeking, I am. The goal is a rising above the mind. I personally did not invent or create this message: it was received. And always it has been received through listening: sometimes in moments of deep meditation, sometimes in periods of initiation, sometimes on the platform while giving lectures and classes, but always while in a state of receptivity. That state of receptivity has been my hidden manna. It is that which has produced all that appears as this message, and all that has taken this message around the world.

As you have learned to work hard and long with the principles of the Infinite Way, so you must learn to stop doing this occasionally, sometimes for a day or two, and say to yourself, "Let me not trust in my mind. Let me relax in God."

When these principles are embodied in you, your Soul begins to feed you. Until you really have that hidden manna, however, keep working with all the principles that are emphasized on every page of the Writings, but do not make this an "eight-hour-day." Take time out to work in the garden, read a good solid book, or perhaps an entertaining novel. Never believe that the Infinite Way is trying to teach you to "mentalize." Mental activity is necessary only when you are learning the truth, when you are feeding consciousness with the letter of truth. We want no Infinite Way student to live by affirmations and denials because that is not living by the grace of God. Invite the Soul! Your Soul overshadows you as you sit, walk, or sleep. Relax in It, without words and without thoughts.

The Spiritual Sabbath

The fruitage of abiding in these principles is a period of rest, and this is the true meaning of the Sabbath. The Sabbath Moses commanded the Hebrews to observe was a period of rest forever. Labor for six days; yes, labor to know these principles; but after the six days of labor you come to a place of Sabbath, which means that for the rest of your days you live by the grace of God, by *My* Spirit. Eventually you come to a place where you realize that *I* is God, and the Word that It imparts to you is your bread, meat, wine, and water. When you have attained a quietness and confidence, you may be sure you have entered the Sabbath.

See what happens on the seventh day: "In the mean while his disciples prayed him, saying, Master, eat. But he said unto them, I have meat to eat that ye know not of."[11] He was telling them not to go out to get meat; but to rest in the Sabbath of *I have:* no words, no thoughts, no might, no power.

You students who are ready for the Sabbath must prepare for it by learning to rest back in this realization: "Let my Soul take over instead of my mind." Then every time you go within, something new and fresh will come forth.

In the consciousness of Sabbath, you need not go out and get meat, for you have it. By what right? By your recognition that you and the Father are one. For six days you have labored to study and to train yourself, and those "six days," remember, are for most of you many, many years. But there comes a rest to *My* people; there comes a Sabbath; and that is when you stop all your metaphysical struggling, relax, and *let* Grace live your life.

When you come to the "sixth day" of your practice, just smile: "I do not have to pray for anything. I already have hidden manna the world knows not of." Do you see how the teaching in the Bible is veiled, and how it takes a transcendental consciousness to unveil it? The mystics did not hide it: words hide it.

Those few students who have been listening and studying with the inner ear must now be entering that period of Sabbath when they can feel within themselves: "I do not know any truth. I cannot live on the quotations of yesterday. The only truth I know is what is coming through today. As far as I am concerned, I am living in the period of unknowing, in which every day I go within to receive the manna for that day, to listen for Thy voice."

A person who is in the Sabbath-consciousness realizes, "Thy grace is my sufficiency for this moment," and he is satisfied. He is resting, not only in the assurance that God's grace is his sufficiency, but that there is a sufficiency of God's grace. In that awareness of Grace, he settles into a consciousness of peace. The "six days" of struggle are over, and today he refuses to labor. Then, whatever is to come through comes through.

The truth found in the Infinite Way is Scripture spiritually interpreted. Because of this, you can go back into your own consciousness and draw out the spiritual interpretation of the passages that come to you. The interpretation may come in a different form from what I have given you, but the principle will be the same.

The Infinite Way takes you through the "six days" of labor—the thinking and knowing of the truth, the searching for truth, pondering truth, meditating on truth—until you go beyond the activity of the mind or intellect. Finally, you come to a place where you can rest in quietness and in confidence because you are now no longer living your own life. Every word that flows from God into your awareness becomes the bread, the wine, and the water. It becomes your health, strength, vitality, and all those things that are necessary for your experience.

"My Doctrine Is Not Mine"

We are on earth but for the one reason of showing forth God's glory, not our own. It was never meant that we should glory in our wisdom, our gifts, or in our skill; but rather that we should recognize that what appears to the world as these are not really ours, but His. "My doctrine is not mine, but his that sent me."[12] So, too, all that the Father has is mine, and I am showing forth

God's glory, not mine. In the message of the Infinite Way, I am speaking God's message, not mine. Whatever shows forth as the prosperity or success of the Infinite Way is not my prosperity or success, but His glory, His grace.

Up until this year, I have never spoken openly of my own spiritual experiences, my initiations, or my contacts with the Infinite Invisible because I know that in the Occident there is no preparation for an understanding of such things. This year, however, I have made no secret of the fact that for eight months I have been under an inner initiation by means of which a higher unfoldment of the Message has been coming through.

Part of my function during this time has been to lift the Infinite Way message itself out of metaphysical language into mystical language, so that our students begin to live only in mystical language, even as we all are trying to live only the mystical life, and yet, not separating ourselves from the everyday business of living because there must always be constructive activity. There must always be business; there must always be all the activities that are going on in the world of a human nature, but they must be lifted up into a higher consciousness. Even though some medium of exchange, such as money, may always be necessary, there can be a greater degree of love and grace in the sharing of its activity. It need not be what is called "cold, hard cash." It can be warm, spiritual cash.

This is written only so that you may know that in your life, in your activity, your business, or your profession, you, too, must realize that the nature of your experience is that God may be glorified, that God may speak through you, sing through you, play through you, or that God may do business through you; but always it is God functioning through and as your individual being.

Crucifying Personal Sense

In all of us, nonetheless, there remains a finite sense of self, which in the last analysis must be crucified. Moses had it in his feeling of his unworthiness. Jesus had it for a great while in his feeling of "I can of mine own self do nothing." I had it definitely in this knowledge that I could not bring forth or carry on the message of the Infinite Way. And each of you has it in the measure that you believe you have a skill, a wisdom, or a talent. In that degree, you still have it, and in the degree that you continue to have it, ultimately that personal sense will have to be crucified, until in the end you can realize, "I do not have any truth; I do not know any truth; I do not have any skill; I do not have any talent: *I* am the truth; *I* am the talent; *I* am the skill." In that moment, humanhood has "died," Christhood has been "born" and revealed in its fullness, and the ascension or transition can take place.

This is repeated in the message of the Infinite Way over and over again in the passages that remind us that it is the personal sense of "I" that must "die," the personal sense of "I" that must be crucified. All our study, all our knowing of the truth, all our healing ministry must eventually lead to the period of Sabbath or Grace, which is the full and complete surrender of self, to the end that God may live on earth as He is living in heaven.

There is then no longer a man in heaven *and* a man on earth; the man who came down and the man who went up are one and the same; the two have become one. There is no longer a kingdom of heaven *and* a kingdom of earth; but the kingdom of heaven is made manifest on earth in oneness. In the realization that *I,* God, is individual consciousness, mine and yours, I turn within so that *I,* God, may reveal Itself through the Word to "I," Joel, as long as there remains an *I,* God and an "I," Joel. When *I,* God, and "I," Joel, can sit in the same chair and commune with each other, this is getting very close to oneness. It is not as close as it will be some day when I ascend unto the Father and thereby become the Father.

Those students who realize that the Infinite Way is a revelation of God Himself appearing on earth, will, of course, understand that the purpose of that revelation is that they may go and do likewise, for "if I go not away, the Comforter will not come unto you."[13] If you keep thinking of this as the demonstration of Moses, Isaiah, Jesus, John, Paul, Joel, or anybody else, you will miss the truth that each one has demonstrated in order to reveal the universal nature of Truth.

How Truth Becomes "Veiled"

What always puts the veil back on the truth that "I AM THAT I AM"[14] is that those who have not yet attained, those who have not yet come into spiritual awareness or the demonstration of their spiritual Selfhood, always love the message so much that they become do-gooders and go out in the world to try to spread it around the world, and they do not have it. Then it becomes lost, because truth can be revealed only by Truth, not by a human being. Truth can be revealed only through the Soul-faculties, not through the mind. Whenever well-meaning persons go out and begin to teach truth through the mind, they are preparing the generation for another period of the absence of God on earth. It is always the do-gooder who gets in the way of spiritual demonstration—the do-gooder or the egotist.

When there is an organization, there are a certain number of persons serving as teachers, and because the demands of organization do not make it possible to wait for those who are spiritually attuned, those closest to that state take over the work. Because the Infinite Way is not organized, that is not necessary. We can be satisfied if we find one, two, three, four, five, or six illumined ones to teach. And if we never have more, it would make no difference, because one, two, three, four, five, or six can do more for the world than ten thousand unillumined.

Therefore, let those who would seek to teach be watchful, and let each person exercise spiritual discernment or discrimination when he seeks to be taught, so he is sure that those who teach are showing forth the fourth-dimensional Consciousness, and not merely some knowledge picked up out of a book. Then we can prevent what has always happened before: the loss of Truth through the ministry of those who have not attained spiritual illumination.

Remember that this rising above the mind, above words and thoughts, does not eliminate the mind, words, or thoughts, but it does eliminate living by them. For example, was there not a day in our metaphysical experience when we lived primarily by affirmations, thereby hoping to bring out harmony? It is true that by our words, by our thoughts of truth, our statements of truth, and our remembrance of truth, we did bring out a measure of harmony; but in the days of the Sabbath and Grace, this is no longer true. We do not live by words or thoughts: we live by Grace.

True, the activity of Grace can come to me as words and thoughts, and then it can be imparted to you in words and thoughts. But I am not living by those words or thoughts, and you are not living by them: we are living by the Grace that produced the words and thoughts. I am living in the Sabbath of resting from declaring words and thoughts to receiving words and thoughts, and letting them flow, filled with the Spirit of God. The Holy Ghost is in them because I did not make them up, I did not arrange them: I let them flow through me. Such words and thoughts are with power. These are the thoughts of God that make the earth melt; these are the words of God that are "quick, and powerful, and sharper than any two-edged sword,"[15] even though they still come through the teacher.

But all you have to do, really, is to remember how many times you affirmed statements of truth because you thought they were going to remove some error or bring forth some harmony, and how many times you have pondered the truth for that same reason, and you will know then that you were living by words and thoughts, sometimes words and thoughts out of books. But not now! Now you live by Grace, and that Grace appears as the message which you may speak or write, and because it is a message of Grace, persons hearing or reading it are healed, and have their lives transformed.

~ 5 ~

RISING TO MYSTICAL CONSCIOUSNESS IN PRAYER AND TREATMENT

In the spiritual life, you must never forget that you are not living your own life and that you have no right whatsoever to consider what you would like to do, when you would like to do it, or how. Always in the back of your mind is the reminder that it is God's life that is being lived, and it is your privilege to be at that state of consciousness where you can watch God live your life without interposing a wish, a will, or a desire of your own.

The average truth student is not at the stage of development where he can do this because he has duties to his family or his business, and until such time as the Spirit Itself says, "Leave all for *Me*," * or "Leave your nets," no student should ever forget his responsibility to his family, his associates, and to his work. Rather should his study and his meditations become the foundation for the more harmonious functioning of these facets of his life.

It is only to the few that the call to leave their "nets" eventually comes, and when it does come, it is unmistakable, and it compels obedience. After that, the nature of one's life changes. This change does not permit the

---

*The word "Me," capitalized or italicized, refers to God.

neglect or desertion of one's business or family obligations, but it does make it possible to provide for their independent care so that one may be set free for whatever demands the call may make. Let no Infinite Way student believe, however, that the call to leave his "nets" is an excuse to desert or neglect his human duties or obligations.

Those who enter the spiritual ministry because of a human desire to do good, or before they have heard the spiritual call, make little or no progress. This is because they have not yet learned to rest on the Infinite Invisible. They do not have the spiritual vision that makes it possible for them to know the Unknowable.

The message of the Infinite Way did not come through the human mind, nor can it be imparted by or to the human mind. To the human mind, this message is as nonsensical as was the Master's command to his disciples to go "without purse, and scrip."[1] A human being would have to know how he could afford to get to his destination, but not so with the spiritual disciple. The spiritual disciple would not stop to question how, when, or where: he would just start traveling. This he could do, however, only if this call came as a true spiritual impulse and out of a developed spiritual consciousness.

The Living of the Spiritual Life Is What Attracts

Through the message of the Infinite Way, it is revealed that God is individual consciousness, our own consciousness, not our human awareness, but a deeper level of awareness than the human. Because this consciousness is spiritual, we can go within—meditate, commune, seek the kingdom of God that is within us, seek spiritual wisdom—and then all the "things"[2] of the world, including whatever is required to perform any spiritual activity given to us or even such things as what to eat, what to drink, and wherewithal to be clothed, will be added to us.

I dare not teach anything as transcendental as that, and I dare not write a book about it until the realization of it is so strong in me that I can turn within, in silence and in secrecy, seeking only the spiritual grace of God, desiring to know only the things of God and letting the Spirit of God bear witness with my Spirit in silence. Then I discover that I have better health, greater happiness, or a sufficiency of supply. When that happens, someone or other is bound to say to me, "Will you teach me?" or "Will you reveal to me what you have discovered?" and eventually a book is written, classes come forth, and then more books. But first of all there has to be the discovery and the demonstration of a principle.

The point is that if I wish to impart anything to anyone that I expect him to believe and to follow, I must have attained some measure of success in the living of it, so that a person who reads and studies my writings has a feeling of rightness about them and a desire to follow this teaching.

If you attain some measure of demonstrable good in your own experience, it is inevitable that sooner or later those associated with you will want to go and do likewise. Eventually, others will learn about it and will want you to share with them what you have discovered that is proving to be good in your life. But it must be understood that you have nothing to impart until you have attained such a consciousness of it that you yourself are showing it forth.

Unlike other religious teachings, the message of the Infinite Way is imparted only through the fourth-dimensional consciousness, or a measure of attained Christ-consciousness. Therefore, the teacher must lift students up to the point where they are able to perceive spiritually because, as human beings, students do not have that capacity. One Infinite Way teacher, lifted to that fourth-dimensional consciousness and thus spiritually endowed, can handle, not only a tremendous ministry, but one which grows until it seems to be almost beyond handling.

God's Holy Temples Revealed in Meditation

The principle is that God is Spirit, and that Spirit is your Spirit. God is infinite consciousness and constitutes your consciousness; therefore, your consciousness is infinite. Knowing this, you must, in a sense, forget the world. In other words, you must not go out into the world seeking your good, but at least for a period, you must refrain from asking or expecting anything, and go within to seek the Kingdom.

In this state of consciousness, it is further revealed that since the kingdom of God is Spirit, that which It has to impart is spiritual. Therefore, to go to It for money, houses, employment, marriages, divorces, or happiness in the human realm is utter nonsense because Spirit knows no such things. God knows only a spiritual universe. So your inner life becomes one of seeking more and more the experience of this inner Grace without trying to translate It into terms of physical health or material wealth, or even human peace on earth. The whole approach is summed up in such questions as: What is the spiritual kingdom? What are the spiritual children of God like? What is the nature of the spiritual temple of God? What is the spiritual household of God? What is spiritual health? What is spiritual prosperity?

The human mind is full of concepts. Its concept of health is that of a painless body, and a heart, liver, and lungs functioning normally. Its concept of supply is that supply consists of money, income, property, or investments. The human mind has many different concepts of home and church. But this will not do. God is Spirit. "Know ye not that ye are the temple of God?"[3] What is the spiritual temple of God? "Know ye not that your body is the temple of the Holy Ghost?"[4]

"Ah, no," you say, "I have seen too many physical bodies in sickness, sin, disease, age, disintegration, and deterioration. Do not tell me that they are temples of God!"

What then is the temple of God? How are you going to find out? Ask "man, whose breath is in his nostrils"[5]? Ask a spiritual teacher? How could he tell you? He knows only what his vision is and what God has revealed to him. But how can he impart that to you? No, it is folly to ask a spiritual teacher what spiritual creation is like. It cannot be told: it can only be experienced. It can be imparted in meditation, but it cannot be expressed in words. Therefore, you must go within; you must go to that which the Master called the "Father."[6] You must go there and, if necessary, plead: "Reveal Thyself. Reveal Thy temple to me, the temple which I am, the temple which my body is, the temple which my family is, the temple which my health is. Reveal these to me. Reveal spiritual Reality."

As long as you have only a human mind with which to receive, you will not get the answers, because "the natural man,"[7] the human mind, cannot receive or know the things of God. Therefore, you must keep seeking, not in the world of men or in the world of books, but in the inner temple of your own being, in that sanctuary where Jesus told us we must go to pray, that inner sanctuary of your own consciousness. You must seek until the activity of the mind is stilled, and the mind settles into peacefulness and quietness, so that in that quietness and confidence you can be still.

When you have attained a state of stillness, something within reveals, *"I* am Spirit," and then you know that you have attained some measure of spiritual discernment, enough of Christ-consciousness so that you can keep on listening for the rest of the message. Eventually, God will reveal Himself, His kingdom, His laws, His temples: temples of health, temples of wealth, temples of love, temples of family, temples of all good, each of which is a temple in the consciousness of God. In fact, each one of these is the consciousness of God formed as a temple.

"My" Peace Brings Freedom from Concern

In seeking spiritual truth, you are seeking only His grace, His love, His life, and eventually that is what you will receive. You will receive His Spirit, which translates Itself as "My peace,"[8] not worldly things, but *"My* peace."

This peace is a freedom from concern, from anxiety, and from fear. You may not recognize it at first, but all of a sudden you realize that you have no more fear, no further concern, no more doubts. *"My* peace," the Christ-peace, has given you a new-found freedom. Now you can be in the world, but not of it. You have none of its fears, none of its doubts, none of its worries. Death is no longer an enemy, since in the realization that God is your life, you can never be separated from life even in death. If God's love is governing you, you cannot be separated from God's love in death, so even the last enemy has been overcome.

Then you recognize that a miracle has taken place: you are no longer just a human being. There is a spiritual Presence within you, a spiritual companion, a spiritual gift, a spiritual Grace, a spiritual peace. There is much more to you now than appears outwardly. To you, this spiritual Presence is the miracle, but strangely enough, the world does not see this as a miracle because it does not even know that it has happened. What the world begins to say is, "Oh, you seem to have better health," or "You have greater supply," or "You have more success in business," or "You have better judgment in investments." To the world, that is the miracle, but to you that is not the miracle: that is the fruitage of the miracle.

The Real Miracle

The miracle is Grace; the miracle is a spiritual inner life that has come to your awareness, that which the Master recognized as "the Father that dwelleth"[9] in him, and which Paul recognized as the "Christ which strengtheneth"[10] him. So the miracle is the attainment of the Christ, but the world does not see this. It says, "What a miracle has happened to you! You have health, wealth, and happiness." And the reason it says this? Because the world is seeking health, wealth, and happiness: it is not seeking the Christ.

You are not of the world if you have sufficiently grasped the principles of the Infinite Way so that you are no longer seeking the health, wealth, or happiness that the world can give you, but are seeking the miracle of inner Grace. Many, at first, do not know that that is what they are seeking, but sooner or later they must learn that they will attain those things they long for only when they stop seeking for them and seek *Me,* the Spirit, the Father within. When they learn that they must turn from seeking the things of the world to seeking the kingdom of God, many of them fall by the wayside. That is why the Master said, "Few there be that find it.[11]. . . Ye seek me, not because ye saw the miracles, but because ye did eat of the loaves, and were filled."[12] Because their whole concern was on the "loaves and fishes," they did not find *Me,* and they dropped away. Only the remnant remained. The remnant remained to say, "To whom shall we go? thou hast the words of eternal life."[13]

You Infinite Way students who through the years have been seeking the one great miracle, seeking with every means that the Infinite Way has offered, you who have left your "nets,"[14] left the seeking of "loaves and fishes"—and by this I do not mean that you have given up your employment or your profession, but that you who have reserved an area of your consciousness for seeking God, even while fishing, making tents, or whatever your outer life may be—you, then, are the ones who must eventually discover this kingdom within, this inner Grace, this *My* peace.

Share with Those in the World at the Level of Their Receptivity

Be still about this great gift of Grace that has been given you; be secretive about it. Do not think that you are called upon to share this Grace with those outside, for you are not to do this until they come seeking It, and then only as you realize that they are seeking It, not the "loaves and fishes." You will never be called upon to go out into the world to proselyte, to save it, or to tell what you know.

I have never been called to that purpose. I have been called only to those who were seeking this Path. They have sent for me, and I have gone. Never yet have I gone to the world; never yet have I gone to the public; never have I been called there. My call has been only to those of my own household, those who were seeking that which I had found.

It is because I have not tried to convince the world that it was wrong or tell it that I had discovered something that is right that I have found no antagonism in the world and no persecution there. What I have discovered is not for the world, until the world realizes that it is a prodigal and that it must seek the Father's house.

Be wise. Learn to live within the sanctuary of your own being and stay there until someone comes to your doorstep; then share with that one to the extent of his capacity to receive, and no further. In proportion as you continue to receive an inner Grace which will be made manifest in a peaceful and happier life, more and more seekers will be led to your state of consciousness to be fed.

This consciousness which you have attained, this state of peace which you have, this inner Grace, which is your meat, your wine, and your water, is also that of those who recognize it and seek it. It is not for the neighbor; it is not even for those members of your family who cannot recognize it. Therefore, it is not offered to them.

Love is offered them at their level of receptivity, but not beyond that. Love, charity, and benevolence are offered to your neighbors, and if their level of receptivity is a check, books, or last year's clothing, then that is the level of love and benevolence you must share with them. But you must not expect that attempting to give them the real meat, the real wine, and the real water which you have discovered will feed them.

Even the same material food that we eat would not really feed people of other nations. Their systems could not take it! Their bodies are not conditioned to it. There are some people who thrive on rice, poi, or fish, but if we tried to give them Napoleons, ice cream, or other delicacies characteristic of the diet of most Westerners, they might not be able to assimilate them. So it is that there is a part of this world that can accept our money, our clothing, and other comforts that we can give them, but they cannot accept the word of God.

Let Your Consciousness Be Prepared to Feed a Hungry World

Once you recognize God as your consciousness and as the substance of your life, you will be wise to let It feed and prosper you, let It appear outwardly as whatever form It may, and then share It with those who seek It, but share the twelve baskets full that are left over with the others.

If you leave the world alone, it will awaken to what you have and want it; but if you try to force truth on the world, you may prevent the world from ever being receptive to it. Such is the nature of the human mind. It rejects that which it does not seek. I am not criticizing or judging anyone or anything: I was in the same boat. I was invited to the "feast"[15] a long, long time before I came. I found my feast in a different direction with a different kind of food, and I had to hunger and thirst until I myself sought the meat that does not perish.

It is inevitable that the world will soon realize that it is the Prodigal, that it is not going to be saved by the tens of thousands of bombs stored away, that it is not going to be fed substantially by the food laid up in storehouses and barns and not available to anybody. The world is even going to recognize that it is not going to be supported by all the gold in Fort Knox, or even by all the gold that is not there. It is going to realize some day that it is not going to be saved by these bombs, nor fed by the reserves of food that never come out of storage until they rot or are burned up.

But do not ever think for a moment that this world right now is not famished. It is famished for that food that is stored where no one can get at it, and it is famished for a sense of safety and security and peace. It is hungering for these things. It is inevitable that just as we have hungered for, and finally found, the Spirit, so the people of the world in their hungering will find it, and fortunate it is—no, not fortunate, because this is the way God operates: "before they call, I will answer."[16] Before they are ready for it, the "banquet" has been arranged, the "feast" has been planned, the "food" has been prepared and set out.

I am sure that never has there been a bit of food created that there was not somebody also created to consume it. So, too, the spiritual feast that is set before the world now will find "banqueters" and "feasters." But all the books of spiritual wisdom in themselves are not sufficient. In the background there must be the "ten"[17] righteous men waiting, tabernacling within their own inner sanctuary, enriching their own consciousness, storing up spiritual treasures, so that when those hungering and thirsting come, there will be those ready to say, "Yes, come and eat. We have storehouses filled, filled and ready, storehouses of Grace."

Then, just as everyone who has come to the message of the Infinite Way has witnessed some measure of fruitage in my life, in my family's life, in our teachers' and practitioners' lives, and in many of our students' lives, so, too, will they come seeking it, the people of this world, and you must be prepared. The real preparation will come forth from the degree of silence and secrecy in which you maintain yourself, because then you will not be wasting your substance on the air, or wasting it by letting it hit up against the human mind that would like to dispute it, argue with you, and discuss it. You will be storing it up, and those who come to you, even though you do not feel led to say a word to them, will feel that inner peace, that inner Grace, and will be fed by it. Even if you say only one word to them, if you give them but one quotation, one passage of Scripture, it will be a whole meal because it will carry with it spiritual consciousness.

When I started in the practice, I gave one hour to every patient who came to me, and at that time it probably took an hour for me to give a patient enough spiritual substance to meet his need; but later, five minutes would do, and still later three minutes. Why? Because it was not the words feeding him: it was the consciousness. As you work in this ministry through the years, your consciousness deepens, and then one word, one quotation, sometimes just a look, a smile, and it is done. Without that consciousness, it may take a whole hour of words.

God is infinite consciousness; God is individual consciousness: yours. God is Spirit; therefore, turn within to your God-consciousness and seek the peace that passes understanding. Seek God's grace which is your sufficiency in all things. Seek His love, and whatever else you may seek, be certain that it is something spiritual. Abide in this Word; abide in this Grace; abide in this peace, never looking to the outside world to see what is going to happen or how it is going to manifest.

Lifting up the Son of God

As long as you live and move and have your being within the spiritual temple of your consciousness, realizing only the presence of spiritual Grace, you are living in and through God, and God is really living as you: you in the Father, and the Father in you—one. You are relaxing your own sense of life that the divine life may take over. This you do silently and secretly, and that which God sees in secret is shouted from the housetops. Not by you—no, by God! It appears outwardly as the forms that the people of the world recognize as good, and this draws them to you, just as the masses were drawn to the Master for loaves and fishes, but ultimately came that they might find His peace, His grace.

In practical experience, this means that when someone comes to you and asks for help for supply, you answer, "No, I cannot work for your supply because you already have an infinity. You think money is supply, but money is not supply. God's grace is supply. Let me give you help to realize that Grace and that peace. Let me give you help to realize the Christ. Let the supply be added, but let us not go to God for supply. Let us go to God for God."

How does one say that to a person? All the money in the world cannot be used as food; even gold mines cannot be eaten. Money is not supply except in the human three-dimensional world, and even then it is here today and gone tomorrow. We are not dealing with money as supply: we are dealing with consciousness as supply; we are dealing with love, gratitude, and benevolence as supply.

When a request comes from someone for help on supply, Infinite Way teachers or practitioners should answer, "Are you referring to money, employment, or property? Please realize that I cannot give you these. I can give you help to lift you higher in consciousness, and if you attain that higher consciousness, you will find the omnipresence of supply in your consciousness, as long as you do not think of supply as money."

In the same way, as patients or students continue to say, "It is my right knee that hurts," or "It is my left ear that aches," the teacher or practitioner should reply, "I understand that, but please remember that spiritual help does not touch the physical body at all. Our work is helping you attain that mind which was in Christ Jesus, in which there is no sin, disease, lack, or death."

Mercifully and gently, not unkindly, turn the patient away from the thought of the health problem to the idea of going within to seek God's peace, "Let us seek spiritual health. Let us seek the temple of God which is your real body."

When someone comes with a tale of unhappy family life, it is so real to him that all he wants is to change his unhappiness to happiness; but as gently as possible, make it very clear, "I cannot give you that without the presence of the Christ, because I do not know how. It is the presence of the Christ that can establish harmony between you and your family. Humanly, I would not know how to do this for you or tell you what to do. In fact, you could give your family all your money, and you would not be at peace with them. You could give them your land, and you might not be at peace with them. You could give in to your wife; your wife could give in to you; and you still would not have peace. But let us go within and tabernacle with God; let us bring God into your family life, and let the Spirit make the adjustment, 'for we know not what we should pray for.'[18] Let the divine Spirit bear witness with our spirit and see if It will not bring peace between thee and thy household."

Persons may keep coming seeking a demonstration of employment, but you have no employment to give. So, for the moment, forget employment, and see if you can receive a message from the Father, because "Man shall not live by bread alone, but by every word that proceedeth out of the mouth of God."[19] Therefore, man shall not live by employment: man shall live by the word of God. Let your work be to bring forth the word of God. Then he will eat and drink and be satisfied, and maybe employed too.

In this way, you will be hastening the day when Infinite Way students will know that the teacher or practitioner is not another branch of *materia medica,* a vice-president of a neighborhood bank, or even a marriage counselor, but that his function is to lift up the son of God in those who turn to him for help.

The Only Goal must Be Attaining
Christ-consciousness

There are many more individuals seeking a spiritual solution to life than there are persons prepared to help them find that way. Even today in the Infinite Way, we are unable to take care of the many demands that come in asking for spiritual help. It would be sad if the world turned to us now, and we had to say, "We are sorry. We know this truth is the answer, but our students have not attained a high enough state of consciousness to give that spiritual help."

After seventeen years? How long does it take? How long does it take a student to attain spiritual consciousness? I can give you half the answer. A student cannot even begin to attain that consciousness until his goal is no longer that of meeting his personal problems of health, supply, or happiness. He must no longer be preoccupied with personal gain. The search for God-awareness must become the primary motive of study. When that is true, then the spiritual student is halfway "home." He must decide that the attainment of Christ-consciousness is his only goal and that having help for his other problems is of secondary importance. I am not saying that anyone should neglect human situations or obligations, but these should be secondary. It then might not take a student too long.

Attaining that mind "which was also in Christ Jesus"[20] should be the primary purpose in life. It is an interesting thing for me to watch this work and see some students who are attaining it beautifully, and then watch those who are seeking a healing for a minor physical claim and complaining because they have not yet attained heaven. In other words, such students are still living for themselves and are making themselves the goal rather than having as their goal the attaining of heaven.

Our concern must be to lift the world into the higher dimension of consciousness where all the "things" of the world are added. "I, if I be lifted up from the earth will draw all men unto me."[21] Let us hurry about this business of being lifted up, so we can lift others into the higher consciousness. Then all problems will solve themselves.

From Metaphysics to Mysticism

The Infinite Way is embarking on the attaining of a higher realm of consciousness in its presentation and demonstration. It is taking the students above the metaphysical and into the mystical, but it is asking them not only to come up out of the metaphysical into the mystical, but also not to burn down the metaphysical temple behind them, any more than they would want to burn down their schoolhouses just because they do not need schools for themselves.

For your own demonstration of spiritual attainment, seek to live "by every word that proceedeth out of the mouth of God." That means to live by turning within to your consciousness and letting your consciousness speak to you, letting the activity of the Christ be your demonstration, rather than the demonstration of employment, supply, happiness, or health.

Those of the present generation have been led up through the metaphysical, where it was legitimate to call for help when their child had a 103 degree fever, and then call up to express gratitude when it when down to

101 degrees, as if we were practitioners of *materia medica*. Or it was legitimate when someone called up and wanted increased supply, and then reported, "Oh, my salary has been doubled!" to consider that a demonstration.

But in the mystical realm, this is not demonstration. The demonstration is the realization of the presence and the activity of the Christ: that is the demonstration. The demonstration is hearing the word of God, because it is This that we live by. The demonstration is the attainment of the meat the world knows not of. The demonstration is the attainment of *My* peace.

This is the point in mysticism at which we have arrived; this is the standpoint from which the Infinite Way has been practiced by those who have recognized this principle. But now it is necessary that every student recognize it, because the world is not going to be saved merely by multiplying the food that is in storehouses and barns, by multiplying the gold in Fort Knox, or by the signing of a peace treaty.

The Demonstration of the Christ

The world will be saved only by the demonstration of the Christ. It may call it "the second coming of the Christ;" but actually the Christ never came and never went, so there is no first or second about it. The Christ has always been present, since God and the son of God have always been one; therefore, the demonstration is not really the second coming of the Christ: the demonstration is our recognition of the *omnipresence* of the Christ. This is the demonstration, our recognition of that which eternally is, eternally has been, and eternally will be.

God is the same forever, from everlasting to everlasting. He changes not; therefore, there has never been a going or a coming. The Christ has always been omnipresent, awaiting recognition, and there have always been individuals to recognize and demonstrate the Christ. But now the Prodigal is no longer an individual; now the Prodigal is the whole of the human world, and today it is the entire human world that thirsts and hungers to get back to the Father's house.

Only through meditation can you go deep down inside your Self, inside your own consciousness, the temple that is within, be at peace, and draw forth the word of God. Otherwise the mind is living out here in the world and is of it, but in meditation it can be in the world but not of it. If, however, you permit your students, your patients, and your friends to believe that you are going to go within for them and draw out a new house, a new automobile, or new employment, you will keep on deceiving them and preventing your own higher unfoldment.

Your higher attainment is really dependent on your not permitting those who come to you to believe that you are going to demonstrate a material universe for them, not even a healthy, wealthy one. It is dependent on the degree in which you can turn them gently away from trying to improve appearances to seeing what the kingdom of God has for them, to what the indwelling Christ has for them, to what manner of temple It can bring forth, and to what happens when the Word is spoken through you.

So, also, the degree of your attainment is dependent on how little you can say to those who come to you, and to what degree you can listen within and let the Voice do the saying–not how much truth you can speak to your friends, students, or patients, but to what degree you can become aware of the Word and let It perform Its work.

We used to think that if we sat with a patient or student and talked with him for a half hour or an hour, we were doing great things for him, and not one second did we let the voice of God come forth, and yet it is the voice of God that really does away with this material world. It is the word of God that we must live by, and all we did was talk to our students and rehash statements of truth, forgetting that it is the word of God that does the miracles, not we, and not any passages we have memorized.

Your own heights of spiritual awareness will depend on your ability to speak to those who come to you for help for five or ten minutes and bring peace to them, and then go within and let the Word come forth, because the more the Word utters Itself within you, the higher your attainment, until ultimately you will not have a voice of your own any more: it will be Its voice, it will be It speaking through you always. This is the mystical height.

~6~

MEASURING SPIRITUAL PROGRESS

For centuries man has lived in a sense of separation from God: he has prayed to a God in heaven, to a God on a crucifix, or to an old gentleman on a cloud. Always he has been taught that God is something separate and apart from his own being, whereas the revelation of every mystic is the profound truth of oneness.

I and my Father are one.   *John 10:30*

He that seeth me seeth him that sent me.   *John 12:45*

Oneness: that is the Master's teaching. There is no twoness. But to believe in oneness is not easy because there is no time in your life when you ever feel that you are God, or when you feel that you are spiritual. Occasionally, you may have a few moments of emotion or ecstasy, or seeming to be on Cloud Nine, but there will always be an hour from then, or tomorrow, when that sense of separation breaks in, and you say to yourself, "I cannot be one with God because I feel so human." Probably you even have a physical pain or a financial lack, and you know that if you were one with God, this could not be.

This failure to recognize your oneness with God arises out of the erroneous teachings that have set up a sense of separation from God and prevented you from taking the necessary steps that will eventually prove that you are one with the Father and that all that He has is yours.

Progress Cannot Be Judged by Appearances

To remedy this misconception of your relationship to God, the first thing that must be remembered is not to judge by appearances. Do not judge by the fact that today you may be very ill or very poor, or that you may be entertaining sinful thoughts or even be committing a sin. Do not judge from any of these things as to whether or not you are one with God. All such conditions can tell you is that at a particular moment you have a sense of separation from God. It does not prove that you are not one with God.

It may be that you will go on being sick for a while, or being poor; it may be that you will go on having carnal thoughts or sinful appetites, and that you might even at times succumb to them. Do not let that fool you, because that, too, is only an evidence of the sense of separation from God, set up during past centuries.

You have not yet attained the actual consciousness of your oneness with God, but the truth is that you are already one with Him. It makes no difference who or what you are: you are still one with God. You will succeed in proving that oneness, however, only in proportion to your attainment of the actual awareness of the relationship that already exists. Therefore, you must not judge by the appearance of today, nor must you try to judge your progress, because no one on the spiritual path can ever evaluate his own progress.

Actually, what happens is that you go along, sometimes for years, feeling that you are making absolutely no progress. There may not be any outer sign of progress, and then all of a sudden, one day or one night, in a split second, as with Saul of Tarsus on the road to Damascus or as with any of the mystics of whom you may have read, it happens.

Every mystic has discovered, as he meditated, studied, practiced, and did whatever he was instructed to do, that in spite of not seeming to make much progress, in one minute of one day, or one second of one night, "whereas I was blind, now I see."[1] The "old man"[2] was dead, and the "new man"[3] had been born.

The reason that you cannot feel any progress in yourself is that you cannot feel spiritual. There is no such thing as a person's feeling spiritual. That is as impossible as feeling that you are honest or feeling that you are moral. You can be honest or you can be moral, but you cannot feel it: you can just *be* it. There is no feeling about it, nor is there any feeling about being spiritual. Being spiritual is a state of consciousness which you are, but you have nothing to compare it with, since the "old man" is gone.

Furthermore, regardless of how spiritual you may become, always there are human traits remaining. "Jesus went into the temple . . . and overthrew the tables of the moneychangers,"[4] which spiritually a Christ would not have done. He called the scribes and Pharisees and the multitudes vipers, which spiritually is a form of malpractice. This was only because in every person—even in the mystic—there is always a trace of his human identity. It is for this reason that you never feel wholly worthy; you never feel that you are really successful or that you are quite making the grade.

It is good that it is so. That was what Paul referred to when he said, "Forgetting those things which are behind, and reaching forth unto those things which are before, I press toward the mark for the prize of the high calling of God in Christ Jesus."[5] Certainly Paul was aware of how far he had to go before he could fully claim Christhood. So you, too, must learn to disregard appearances. You must learn to disregard the many days when you will feel very human, when you will have reason to think that you are failing. You must ignore all that.

Signs of Spiritual Progress

There is a way, however, of measuring the degree of progress you are making on the spiritual path. That way is not by trying to see how much more spiritual you feel, how much better you are behaving, or how much more virtuous you are. These are not the signs.

No, it is in your reactions to what is presented to you as pictures of the world that the signs of spiritual progress can be found. For example, to read of wars, threats of wars, and other horrors, and discover that the fear those things engender in you is lessening because of your realization that temporal power is not power is a definite sign of spiritual progress. The less you react with fear to the sins and the diseases of the world, the greater the degree of spiritual progress you have made and are making.

In proportion as you understand that temporal power is not power in the presence of God, there will be less and less reaction to the pictures of disease or accident presented to you. Newspapers almost daily report the lack of food and other necessities in many countries in the world. If, instead of reacting to these accounts with horror or with pity, you can realize that lack of any kind is a universal belief because supply is spiritual and, therefore, omnipresent, you may help to lift those who are entertaining a material sense of supply out of such hypnotism.

There is an infinity of supply, and this realization on your part is not only an indication of your own spiritual progress, but also a help in removing lack and limitation universally. Through your meditation, somewhere, somebody wakens to the truth that there is in reality no lack of supply. What there is, is a mistaken concept of supply. In other words, those who experience lack are entertaining a physical or material sense of supply.

If only a few persons realized that supply is spiritual, that the grace of God constitutes supply, and that because there cannot be any place where God is not, there cannot be any place where Grace is not, they would then awaken some of the sleeping souls to the apprehension of this truth, and in one way or another, supply would begin to flow. Probably those who are holding on to supply in warehouses and cold-storage plants would in a measure be touched by this spiritual light and release the form or material sense of supply because even materially there is no lack of supply in the world. There is enough in the ground and enough stored away to take care of everybody. There is merely an absence of the realization that the necessities of life do not have to be hoarded in warehouses and barns, because they are the flowing grace of God.

Furthermore, once you begin to perceive that there is no such thing as an evil man or woman because evil is not a man or a woman but an impersonal temptation or tempter, then, when you witness evil men and women, instead of reacting with condemnation, a smile comes inside of you with a "Father, forgive them their ignorance"—not their evil, their ignorance. They could not be evil if they were not ignorant. Therefore, you do not feel horror at the evils or the evil persons of the world, but a compassion, a "Father, forgive them; for they know not what they do."[6] Such an attitude is a sign of spiritual progress.

Another sign of spiritual progress is the extent to which you pray for your enemies. The longer you see them as human beings, the longer there will be something to be forgiven or to be prayed over. There is only one way to pray for your enemies, and that is to understand that God is individual being. The more you realize that, the fewer mistakes they can make, and the fewer sins they can commit. But the more you look upon them as human beings who are sinning and whom you in your generosity are going to forgive, the more egotistical you are, and the more you bind them.

If you have surrendered yourself to God, so that you have no Self but that Self which is God, and know that whatever of good, emanating from you or through you, is of God and whatever of error is just your inability to let God fully function, then you must know that this is the truth about everybody, whether or not he is aware of it.

But if he is not aware of this truth, how is he to become aware of it? And I can tell you that no one can ever become aware of this truth by himself because the human mind that functions in him is not going to give itself up. It is only as you pray aright, that is, as you, in your meditation, realize, "All that Thou art, I am," that a person can be touched by the Christ which you are loosing in the world. This can change him, and only this. It has been so with me, and it will be so with you.

What actually counts in measuring your spiritual progress is your motive. Is there a drive keeping you on this Path until you attain God-realization? Is there something holding you to your meditation, your study, and to the practice of spiritual principles? If there is something holding you to these spiritual disciplines, you are making progress. But it is not really you making progress: it is a sign that you have been touched by the Spirit, and It is not going to let you go until It breaks through fully.

Only a Touch of the Spirit Can Bring You to the Path

But how and why did an activity of the Christ touch your consciousness? How did it happen that you came to the spiritual path? It is an error to believe that you are on this path by some virtue of your own. No human being ever gets such a longing for God. Whether you want to believe it or not, the truth is that in your humanhood you could not have come to a spiritual teaching. You would have gone on forever and forever in your ritualistic practices or in some mental abracadabra. You are on the Path now only because at some period of your life you were inwardly touched, and you found yourself turned in a direction which you could not have taken by yourself, because it called upon you to abandon the faith of your fathers, to abandon the friendships and relationships that you had developed.

You have had to learn to have a secret of your own within, hidden from your friends and relatives. As a human being, you do not have the capacity to do that, any more than your friends who are still functioning on the human level of life have that capacity. You only know that you were directed and what happened after you were directed. You do not know what it was that made it possible for you to open a book and feel, "Ah! this is it! I must follow it; I must go further." Ninety-nine other persons could open the same book and see nothing in it. If the power were in the book, then those ninety-nine would also find it in that same book, but the power is not in the book: the power is in consciousness.

But what was it that prepared your consciousness to be able to follow a spiritual path, and sometimes follow it through a great many difficulties? What, but Grace? You do not know whether at some moment or other in your experience you opened yourself with a sort of "Oh, God," or whether someone else's praying reached your consciousness. It may have been someone on this side of the "veil," or it may have been someone on the other side of the "veil," because every mystic who has ever lived is still alive and praying. Not one of them is dead: Moses is not dead; Elijah is not dead; Jesus is not dead; John is not dead; Paul is not dead–and they are not interested in billiards, bowling, baseball games, or football games. They are still alive, spiritually alive; and if they are in your consciousness, it could be that their prayers reached you–or it could have been the prayers of some mother, grandmother, or great-grandmother, praying in what we call the "beyond," that have touched you.

You do not know where the Spark came from that made you leave your "nets."[7] And do not forget that in the degree that you have left your old pattern of life and the religious concepts of your forebears, or that you have let relatives and friends drift out of your life because of new associations on the spiritual path, in that degree you have left your "nets," you have left your old mortality.

Surely you must recognize that you could not have done this of yourself. If it had been possible, then the three and a half billion others who are out in the world would be doing the same thing, because you may be assured that there is not a person living who does not want the *effects* that come as the fruitage of a spiritual way of life. At the present time, most of them do not want the way in which it came to you because they have no knowledge of that way, and if they had, to them it would seem dull, monotonous, and dreary. But be assured that they all want peace of mind, peace of Soul, a healthier physical body, and a more intelligent mind. They want a greater assurance of God's grace in the world because they are all living in the fear of bombs and wars, which fear they would lose if they had any assurance at all of God's grace.

Millions want what those on the spiritual path have found and if they had the capacity, they would be on that Path; but they do not and cannot have the capacity until the Spark touches them. That Spark may come through your prayers, or it may come through the prayers of those whose lives are dedicated to meditation whether on this or on the other side of the "veil."

Do you really think that the Spirit of God makes us in some degree a light to others and then puts out that light? Impossible! I am convinced that no spiritually illumined person has ever died. True, each one in his turn passes from our physical sight because that is inevitable. How would it be possible for anyone to remain on earth forever in the monotony of human beingness? Therefore, there must be a progressively unfolding experience. But would it not be distressing to think that the ten, twenty, thirty, or forty years that you have given to a spiritual study and activity all ended because you passed on? I cannot accept that; I just cannot accept it!

Surely, you cannot believe that the spiritual function of Jesus stopped at the Crucifixion, the Resurrection, or the Ascension, or that the great contribution Buddha made, or the contributions made by John, Paul, or by thousands of others ceased when they stopped breathing. What do you believe about yourself? Do you believe that all the devotion and the dedication you have given to your spiritual study is going to come to an end?

I am sure that the reason the Master said, "Lay not up for yourselves treasures upon earth, where moth and rust doth corrupt . . . But lay up for yourselves treasures in heaven where neither moth nor rust doth corrupt,"[8] was because he knew that while you leave all your material possessions at the probate court, you take the spiritual treasures with you wherever you go.

What do you do with them? When you leave this plane of existence you really do not go any place. Life is an activity of consciousness; it is lived in consciousness, and you never escape out of consciousness. You continue to pray and meditate, and anyone anywhere who is receptive and responsive comes under the influence of that prayer and meditation.

There is nothing of which I am quite so certain as the truth that Moses, Elisha, Elijah, Buddha, Jesus, John, and Paul are still about their Father's business, and even though you and I may be lesser lights, as we go into a higher domain, we too continue functioning. By now, however, you should have reached the stage where you are no longer interested in laying up the treasures that you have learned are going to be taken from you. Therefore, you will no longer even bother to lay them up: you will now give your first attention to spiritual matters.

The spiritual treasures that you have laid up in your consciousness walk right out of here with you. In fact, that is what makes you, you. You are what you are by virtue of your attained spiritual consciousness, and you will be greater than you are in the measure of your greater attainment of spiritual consciousness. Never believe that any condition or circumstance is going to bring your life to an end or end your service to God or man. What God is storing up in you as spiritual treasures, you are not only going to give back here on earth, but you will give back in multiplied experiences when you have dropped whatever material sense of existence you still carry.

Once you have been touched and there is the certainty that this is your path, you must not look back. Now, of course, that is fairly easy if you look at it one way because when this Light touches you, you can no more look back on the things that you once thought were pleasures and profits because the degree of the Spirit that you have attained has wiped that out. You never again can be completely enthralled by the things of the flesh; you never again can be wholly satisfied by the profits of the pocketbook. Once a person is touched by the Spirit, those things become only incidental; but do not be misled or overly confident: there is still the possibility of fearing the things that you have always feared.

The Last Enemy on the Path

The one great fear everyone has is the fear of death. "The last enemy that shall be destroyed is death."[9] You may not agree with that, but it is undoubtedly true that in all human souls there is a fear of death. Oh, they may deny it! But whether they are conscious of it or not, ever present is that fear of the inevitability and finality of death. It may not be a fear of any horror awaiting them. It may be just a fear of the unknown or the fear of leaving comfortable or familiar places, just as always there have been people who migrated to new countries, while others stayed behind because they would rather endure their present misery than risk the promise of the unknown.

Sometimes I think that fear of the unknown, that is, fear of death, influences even those who have gone some distance on the Path. The miseries of human life, instead of releasing them, tend to keep them here because what lies ahead is a mystery. The things that might ultimate in death, therefore, bring about a fear that could hold them back in their spiritual progress.

At some time or other, we all must overcome the fear of death and come to the realization that what looks like death is not actually death: it is a transition into a different state of experience, similar to what happens when the caterpillar becomes a butterfly. I suppose the caterpillar thinks it dies, but actually it does not: it becomes a butterfly. So it is that we do not really die, regardless of what the appearance may be: we make a transition into another phase of life. When we under-stand that, the fear of death is gone because for us it is not death any more.

You must face the fact that eventually you are going to leave this present phase of life and enter another one, about which, at the present time, you know very little. But if you understand this experience as a transition, you will lose your fear of death, and when you have completely, really and honestly, lost your fear of death, you are wholly on the spiritual path and you will have arrived at least at the entrance to heaven. But you cannot reach this stage until you have realized that God is your Selfhood. Then the life you are living is God: God living your life, and, of course, you are perfectly willing for God to take it around the world or even into the next world, since it is His life, not yours.

God gave Himself to this world as you, the begotten Son. He did not breathe into you your life: He breathed into you His life, His breath. So it is not your breath you are breathing: it is His breath; it is not your mind through which you are thinking: it is His mind; it is not even your body through which you are functioning: it is the temple of the living God.

The more you realize this and surrender yourself, that God may function as your mind, your Soul, your life, your breath, your being, and your body, the more of divine Grace will be expressed as you. While those ignorant of this truth may tell you how wonderful you are, how noble, or how beautiful, you will be saying to yourself, "How I wish you knew that this is not I you are looking at, but 'he that seeth me seeth him that sent me,' for I and the Father are one." This can come about only when you have surrendered yourself to the extent that you are not trying to manipulate or influence God with your mind, not even in your behalf, and certainly not in your neighbor's behalf; but when you are accepting God as the Being of every being, and then letting God function.

God Is

Through the principles of the Infinite Way, you have learned that you cannot influence God, and if you know in advance that no matter what thoughts or words go through your mind, they are not going to influence God, you will stop thinking thoughts and words. It is only as long as you believe that your words and thoughts are going to reach God and have some influence with Him that they continue. As soon as you realize that all these attempts to influence God are just a waste of time, your thoughts will come to a stop, and your prayer will be a receptivity, a listening, an awaiting God's grace, a waiting for the still small voice, and then that Spirit of God enters your consciousness, consciously, and you become aware of It.

Does anyone know what God is? Has the mystery of how this world came into being ever been solved? When you look up into the sky at night and see the stars, the moon, and the planets, can you fathom what produced their glory? Does anyone know? Who can know what Infinity is? Who can know what God is? But as you look at this orderly universe of sun, moon, stars, planets, and tides, and the immutable law of nature that makes apples come from apple trees, that makes two times two four, and that makes do-re-mi music, how much farther can you go than to realize that since man did not create this, certainly you know that God is?

To go any further than this is to set the mind working, and thereby to create a barrier between you and God. Having acknowledged that God is, you have gone as far as the deepest religionist has ever gone. Even when he observes all the sacraments and all the holy days, he does no more in these observances than to say, "God is." I say, "God is," without going through any of the forms. I not only say it but, more than that, I sit back and let God be God to me, and not merely a form of worship in the mind. I am finished with "God is" in half a second, and get back into my silence where I open myself to God: "Speak, Lord; for thy servant heareth."[10]

In that one statement I have worshiped God, I have acknowledged the infinite nature of God, the omnipresence, omnipotence, and omniscience of God. I have done all that without a word except "Speak, Lord." What would I expect God to speak to me if not power, intelligence, love? Thus, having acknowledged God, I am as devout as the most religious person on the face of this globe. No matter how many words anyone uses or how many acts he performs, he has done no more than acknowledge God, and I have done that.

But I am going to do one additional thing. I am going to stop being "me." I am going to stop pretending, and I am going to let God take over my life and live it. I am not going to make any pretense about being good or being spiritual; I am not going to make any pretense about being charitable or benevolent because at best all my charities and all my benevolences are limited to comparatively small amounts. Never do I give all my resources away, so I cannot be quite as charitable or benevolent as sometimes I might like to think I am. I am charitable and benevolent only to the extent that I can let God function through me, and if I could let It function through me more fully, I could be more charitable and more benevolent and more loving and more patient. But at least in the degree that I can, I am making no pretense about Joel, and I am making no claims for him.

That Which Sent the Infinite Way into Expression

Those of you who have known me throughout my entire experience in this work know that I have never claimed to have a great understanding, because if there is anybody in the world who knows I do not have it, it is I, myself. My understanding has always been completely limited to whatever has come through in any given moment, and whatever I knew yesterday was yesterday's manna, and it is not doing me any good today. Only that which I know this minute represents my understanding; and it is not even mine, really: it is God's gift to me. Once I have surrendered myself, there is not God *and* "me": there is God functioning through me. "I live; yet not I, but Christ liveth in me."[11]

Only in the degree that you can give up the intellectual exercise of trying to know and worship God with the mind, and instead live in the constant atmosphere of "Thank You, Father! You are my very being. You live my life," and keep yourself sufficiently clear so that you are always the transparency through which God's grace flows, is there no ego, no personal self, and no attempt at personal attainment. This may not be easy, but it is essential to spiritual progress.

This must be as clear to every student as it is to me in connection with the Infinite Way because if the Infinite Way were mine, it would have its limitations: it would have had a beginning and it will have an ending. But if the Infinite Way is God's message being expressed in human consciousness, it will be there for eternity.

No one knows as completely as I do that this whole activity and message of the Infinite Way is Truth expressing Itself, God's grace and God's glory being revealed in human consciousness. It must be evident to any Infinite Way student who has been with us even seven or eight years that no human being could have brought through this message or have witnessed its establishment throughout the world purely through his human wisdom or powers, and certainly not unless there were a tremendous checkbook behind him, high-powered advertising, and other forms of promotion. Therefore, to witness what our students have witnessed must be evidence to them that there is *something* functioning behind the message and behind the messenger. Unless this is clear, I do not see how anyone can account for all that we have witnessed in this work.

It has been my particular saving grace that I have known from the beginning that this message is something that keeps coming through me from an invisible Source. It must be from the true Source because of its fruitage. Nobody has been harmed or impoverished by the Infinite Way, and those who have been open and receptive and responsive to it have been spiritually healed: physically, mentally, and financially. Therefore, it cannot be of man: it must be of God.

If it is of God, Joel is not responsible for what happens to it: he is responsible only for maintaining himself as a transparency; nor is he responsible for what happens to the Infinite Way when he is no longer physically present because That which sent it into expression will continue to function it. No one is ever going to tamper with the Infinite Way because it has no personal savior or personal revelator. It is the spirit of Truth Itself voicing Itself, and be assured that the voice of Truth will always have a transparency, or a million transparencies, through which and as which to reach human consciousness.

The Master emphasized that the message he gave the world was not his, but the Father's that sent him. That is the reason a simple Hebrew rabbi could be instrumental in giving forth a teaching that has endured through the ages, and which probably is only now being recognized in its fullness. Therefore, you must agree that behind the Master, there must have been That which not only expressed the specific principles he taught, revealed, and imparted, but gave him the power, courage, and wisdom to stand in the face of the entire church of his day until the message could be so established in consciousness that he could say, " 'My words shall not pass away'[12]– everything else may, but not *my* words." So it has proved to be.

Watching What God Has Wrought

Some of you have surely noticed when I have been in class how sometimes my head has turned to one side. That is when I have become aware of the Presence. When that happens, then I am no longer aware of myself as a teacher on a platform: the Presence takes over and does the work; and there are no longer two: there is only one.

It is that same way in meditation and treatment. At first, there is a "me" listening for the still small voice, a "me" inviting God to speak; but then, as I get into that listening attitude, this "me" disappears, and all there is, is that Presence fulfilling Itself. If somebody is healed, It is doing it; if somebody is benefitted, It is doing it; if somebody becomes aware of the Presence through the principles of the Infinite Way, It is doing it: this hidden manna, this Presence. It is the secret meat of which the Master spoke. He, too, was aware of a Presence, which he called "the Father within." For a long while he knew that there was an identity called Jesus, but he was also aware of the Father within, the Presence. That was his hidden manna; that was the meat the world knows not of: that was the grace of God within him.

So you must stop thinking of your life as yours and begin to think of it as God's life. In periods of deep meditation, more especially when the work is for others or for the world, you will reach a state when there is no more "you" to you. To the outer world there is a "you," but now you are aware that this "you" is not living your life, but that it is the Presence that is doing it, this Grace. The "you" has completely disappeared, and the Presence is all there is.

There is not God *and* you: there is only God. That is why Jesus could say, "Inasmuch as ye did it not to one of the least of these, ye did it not to me," [13] God, because "the least of these" also is God. But it is only in the highest moments, when the selfhood called "me" or "you" completely disappears that the spirit Itself is living the life.

I do not know what would happen to anybody if he ever attained that state of consciousness and maintained it on earth forever. It is an experience that comes in moments of illumination, but for the greater part of my life I have found that it is as if there is still a Joel, and he is pretty empty. He, himself, has no qualities of goodness, because it is the Father working through him, but neither has he any qualities of evil, because if there is any evil that comes through, it is a momentary world hypnotism. He has no evil and he has no good: he is living always with those ears open in an expectancy, and then whatever comes through is God's presence and God's grace, and the rest, what the world calls a human personality, remains, you might almost say, a nothingness. It is really a nothingness because it has no desire: it does not want to be any place in particular; it does not want to do anything except what it is doing and what is being done through it; it has no hopes, no ambitions, and is not seeking to achieve anything.

Behold the Spirit Functioning as Your Life

The goal of the mystical life is to be a beholder of God in action, a life in which nothing is ascribed to one's self, not even good motives. As for desire, there is none. There are not even needs because every need seems to be met before one becomes aware of it as a need. This is living by Grace, but you can live fully by Grace only as that selfhood, that which has a desire, a hope, or an ambition, disappears.

Then life is wholly lived by Grace because It functions to Its end, not your end and not my end. If I had something to pray for, it would mean that I have an end; but I have nothing to pray for because I have no end, I have no object in life.

I have only this minute to live, this minute in which I must be fulfilled by the Spirit; and if I have a tomorrow, it will be the same life. Whether it is being lived in California, South Africa, England, or on some other plane, it will not be any different from the life that I am living here and now; and furthermore, I will not be in some particular place because the desire is to be there rather than some other place, but because I have been sent. I do not desire to be any place except where I am sent.

It is in the degree of our desirelessness, in the degree of our selflessness, our unselfedness, that the mystical life is lived. That is what the mystical life is: it is attaining that consciousness where you find yourself living every day, but not wondering about tomorrow because there is no tomorrow for you: there is tomorrow only for God.

Once you have chosen the mystical or spiritual path, you have no power to be either good or evil because when you meditate and make contact with the Spirit within, It performs that which is given you to do. It lives your life, and It is neither good nor evil: It is just spiritual, perfect, and infinite. There is no such thing as good or evil in Spirit; there is no such thing as rich or poor in Spirit: there is infinity. There is no such thing as health or sickness: there is immortality.

When you are not living by bread alone, by exercise or diet, when you are not depending solely on money, property, or investments, but when you are living by the word of God that you contact in your meditation, you are no longer living according to your will to be good, to be charitable, or your will to be moral. This is no longer your choice; this no longer lies within your power.

Every time that you go within, touch the Spirit, and feel a release, that Spirit is performing the functions of your life, and whatever function you have to perform will be infinitely good, and it will be for eternity, not just for today or tomorrow, and not torn down next week or next month by a depression, a boom, or a war. In other words, the evils of this world will not come nigh your dwelling place because it will no longer be your dwelling: it will be the Father within doing the dwelling. Do you see why it is that when you go to God, it can be only in a complete surrender?

Progress on the spiritual path seems to come slowly and imperceptibly, but years of devotion, dedication, and persistence inevitably bring the goal of conscious oneness with God closer and closer. Your pure motive leads you to where there is less and less reaction to the appearance-world; forgiveness and a lack of condemnation mark your attitude toward your fellow man; the fear of death diminishes; and the ego or personal sense is superseded by a recognition of the divine Self of you and of all men. "He that seeth me seeth him that sent me."

~7~

WORLD WORK FOR ALL
INFINITE WAY STUDENTS

Most persons in the world are confident that ultimately there will be a good world, and that either the
evolution of human consciousness or just the passing of
time will make it so. In this belief they are "barking up
the wrong tree," because human consciousness is built
on self-preservation as its first law, and therefore, the
longer human consciousness evolves, the more ways it
is going to find of preserving itself at somebody else's
expense.

As you well know, the world has not been saved in all
these thousands of years; and if it is to be saved, it will
not be by human consciousness evolving to the point of
making bigger and better bombs or forming bigger and
better organizations. No, if the world is to be saved, it
will be by the activity of the Christ in human consciousness, and this activity will eventually erase human
consciousness, so that no longer will self-preservation be
the first law of human nature.

Certainly all those on the spiritual path are discover-
ing that they are experiencing fewer of the world's
problems and that they are better enabled to meet those
problems. But Infinite Way students who engage in
prayer and meditation for themselves and for their
families must go beyond their immediate circle and set

aside a little time for the rest of the world. Probably some students may not have thought this important because they are so certain that the world is going to be saved.

The world, however, is really a world made up of individuals, and just as each one of us could go on being a human being from the cradle to the grave and still die a human being, so, too, can the whole world go on the same way. It is because the activity of the Christ has touched our individual consciousness in some measure that we find ourselves to a degree free of the world's problems.

It is only when a person has been touched by that which is transcendental, by that which is spiritual, that he can even begin to approach the goal set by Paul in his statement, "I live; yet not I, but Christ liveth in me,"[1] or by the Master when he said, "I can of mine own self do nothing.[2] . . . The Father that dwelleth in me, he doeth the works."[3]

The Study and Practice of Principles
Lift Consciousness

In the early years of our study of the Infinite Way, we must abide by the specific principles of this message very closely and very intensely. The study and practice of these principles lead us to the point where we no longer hate, fear, or love the human scene and develop our consciousness to that place where we realize the nonpower of what the world calls power and we come to recognize that there is *something* greater than ourselves functioning within us.

As we progress in this work through study and practice and as some measure of the Spirit of God enters our consciousness, we find ourselves called upon to help others. The others may not know why they come to us, but they do come; and when they ask for our help, generally we can give it because by the time that they come asking for help, we have attained sufficient spiritual endowment to make it possible for us to give them the help they seek.

We, of ourselves, could never do the things that many of us are often called upon to do. We, of ourselves, could not help a person overcome a serious disease, lose his sins and false appetites, or mold a new disposition. There is nothing about us, as human beings, that would ever make it possible for us to do that for another. Divine Grace would not allow anyone to call on us until we are prepared.

Therefore it is our function never to want to give help, never to want to be in the healing ministry, never to want to do anything but perfect ourselves, study, meditate, and let our consciousness become so filled with the activity of the Christ that in a certain moment It breaks out, and then, somebody comes and asks for help, and that starts us on our way.

Eventually a great truth begins to dawn in the consciousness of every student of spiritual wisdom regardless of his approach: If This that functions through me as a blessing to myself and others is so powerful, can It not then help the entire world? If I can pray for my neighbor and my neighbor benefits by my prayer, can I not then pray for the entire world?

Praying for the world has been going on for centuries, and it is true that a great deal of that praying, both in the visible scene and in the invisible scene, has had and is having an effect upon mankind. But only as we rise higher in the understanding of prayer will we witness a greater fulfillment of spiritual peace and spiritual harmony on earth.

Evidences of Evolving Consciousness

Looking at the world from the standpoint of the consciousness of mankind, we must admit that the world is better today than it was a century ago, even though there are still areas of consciousness in which much room for improvement is needed, such as man's inhumanity to man, the threat of atomic bombs, the continued slavery of one kind or another, or the domination of one people over another. But let us put it this way. Today there is far less inclination to go to war than there was forty years ago; there seems to be less reason to stage the vicious strikes that disrupted our industrial life; and there is a greater inclination on the part of mankind to care for the less fortunate. In my own lifetime, orphanages and homes for the aged were horrible places. Orphans were put on farms where they had to do hard manual labor. They were worse off than servants: they were really slaves, let out to families to be household drudges. Much of this has been done away with, and what remains is rapidly being changed.

In my younger days, all that a workman had to look forward to when he reached the age of fifty or sixty and was physically incapacitated was either to be supported by his children or to be sent to a home for the indigent. There were no benefits provided for him by the government or by industry, and much less was known of unemployment compensation and old age insurance. All this has been changing. Consciousness is at a higher level today than it was even fifty years ago, and far greater than a century ago.

These attainments, great as they are, are not sufficient. Humanity is now faced with the question of survival. Therefore, everyone who has attained enough spiritual endowment to help relieve individuals of their pains, sins, diseases, lacks, and limitations must inevitably turn to the larger subject of world work, or praying for the world. In carrying on this work, it must be remembered that we do not pray that our enemies be defeated and that our allies achieve victories. We do not pray for the Republican Party, the Democratic Party, or the Socialist Party, because all such prayers bring us down to the level of attempting to improve the human scene in terms of our own human judgment of what is good and right.

In order to pray aright, we must not pray for any earthly condition. Even though we might believe that we have a plan which would save the world, we do not pray for its success. There never has been a man on earth so good that he would know how to make laws which would benefit everyone. No one has ever been that intelligent. Since humanhood is based on the law of self-preservation, nothing of a human nature will save the world.

Have we not all seen good men become bad, and intelligent men who have lost their intelligence? We have all known good human beings, but unless those good human beings have been activated by the Spirit, seldom have we witnessed them working impersonally and impartially for the good of everyone. And because that is true of human beings, that is the reason for the failure of the League of Nations and may bring about the failure of the United Nations. Each representative is working primarily for the interests of his country, his race, or his religion.

Intelligent World Work

Praying for the world does not mean praying for peace on earth because that is praying for an effect. We can pray only that the kingdom of God be realized on earth as it is in heaven, and then that realization will bring peace.

If, through our experiences with a spiritual message, we have had some proof that in the presence of the Christ the carnal mind is not power, then we can go on to the greater realization that the carnal mind is the "arm of flesh,"[4] or nothingness. If we can become convinced that the carnal mind is a nothingness, we should have no trouble at all in engaging in world work because, whether it is manifesting as one individual or as a billion individuals, there is only one carnal mind. When we can perceive that the carnal mind is nonpower in the realization of the presence of the Christ, we are helping nullify it for the world.

It is not enough to know that the carnal mind is not power. We must know that it is only in the realization of the presence of the Christ that it is not power. The carnal mind is power on its own level of action. Those who want to drop bombs will drop them, unless and until the activity of the Christ stops them. Nothing else is going to stop them. It is only when this carnal mind comes into contact with the Christ, with our individual Christ-consciousness, that it is proved to be of no power. Wherever Jesus moved with his Christ-activated consciousness, sin, disease, and death disappeared on his coming. So, too, it is with each one of us. Wherever we move with some measure of spiritual endowment, some measure of sin and disease must dissolve.

"Ten" Righteous Men Can Nullify the Carnal Mind

Since we are in agreement that there is but one carnal mind, there is no reason why "ten"[5] righteous men should not nullify the carnal mind for the whole world. Everyone is not receptive, but fortunately we do not have to wait for everyone. We need be concerned only with the realization that the activity of the Christ in our consciousness dispels the carnal mind.

When I engage in spiritual work, it is not for the purpose of changing any set of human circumstances. My only interest is the realization of the activity of the Christ dissolving mortal sense. Remember, there is only one claim, the claim that the carnal mind has power and that it not only can have evil power, but sometimes it can even have good power.

All the movements set in motion in the world today for racial betterment and equality are the result of a spiritual activity. There have always been those who knew that there is only One, and because of those few, there has been a righteous prayer to stir up the racial situation and eventually lead us into the tomorrow of oneness. What you witness in the form of parades and demonstrations is really the carnal mind trying to be good; but it is not being good because it will not bring freedom. Freedom, equality, and justice are brought about only by a change of consciousness. So the real workers will work behind the scenes by realizing the activity of the Christ, dissolving human beliefs, human theories, and human antagonisms.

If we were to pray to remove the sins of our friends, relatives, or community, and if we succeeded, what would be attained? The human mind is still there and is always fertile ground to take on more sins, and so tomorrow we would have to pray to remove those sins. That is why the Master taught that if one error is removed, we may be making room for seven more to enter. So we are not really setting out to make man better and we are not praying that he lose his sins: we are praying that the activity of the Christ take over his consciousness. When it does, there is no sin left in it because there is no room for sin in the Christ-mind.

What Is Racial Equality?

What a price was paid in the Civil War to free the Negroes, and how little freedom that war really brought! Do you not see that the carnal mind was operating on the side of both the North and the South, operating as both good and evil? Had God entered that scene, there would have been freedom, and there would not have been the lag in cultural and economic opportunity that exists in the South today between the Negroes and the white population. Because of that lag, if we lived in a Southern town of ten thousand persons and eight thousand of these persons were Negroes with little or no education, it is understandable that we would have difficulty granting them equality.

Then what is the answer? If we are praying spiritually, we will not be called upon for a solution to those problems: we are called upon only for the recognition of the reign of the Christ. Then we will see the matter taken care of, and there will be a transitional change.

The world must face the fact that the black and yellow races are in the majority, and the day may soon be at hand when they control this entire world on the basis of numbers. The only way to prepare for this is to provide education, cultural advantages, and opportunity for spiritual unfoldment for the African and the Asiatic peoples, so that we can all meet in equality in the deliberative assemblies of the world or in our own Congress and rejoice in it.

Had the education of the Negro and his cultural development begun on a mass scale after the Civil War, who would care today if he did vote in the majority? Who in Hawaii cares that the Japanese are voting in the majority? Who cares? Nobody cares, because the Japanese have reached a certain point of education, culture, and spiritual endowment. But think what objection there would be if this were happening and the Japanese were at the cultural, educational, and spiritual level of many of the Negroes in the South who have been denied the opportunity to develop themselves. So can you not see that it is really not who votes or who votes in the majority, if we are all equally well-educated, cultured, and of spiritual endowment? That is when we will witness a United Nations that can vote effectively because countries educationally, culturally, and spiritually un-endowed will not be voting in the majority.

When the activity of the Christ takes over, in a generation or two it will bring about complete equality. Then no one will really care what ethnic or racial group is governing our city or our country because the dedication and devotion of any of them would be basically the same. We have no better example of this in the world than in Hawaii, where, at this writing, there is one Chinese and there are two of Japanese descent in the halls of Congress, and nobody questions their patriotism or capacity to represent their state. No one questions their intelligence, and no one questions their culture. Why? Because the equality is not merely one of lip service. They are the equals of anyone in their education, culture, and their spiritual endowment, and for that reason nobody is concerned that three of our representatives from Hawaii are of Asiatic descent. This is a very great lesson to remember. What difference would it make if eventually everybody in Congress were a Negro or an Oriental, if they all had the basic patriotism, education, culture, and spiritual endowment? Would it make any difference? Of course not!

For years and years, the Jews have lived in the United States as a minority, and they have been governed almost entirely by Protestants and Catholics, and this has not caused any friction. The Negroes have lived as a minority in the North under the government of the white population, and they have steadily improved their economic, educational, and cultural status.

The whole subject of race relations and religious prejudice is being tackled from the wrong angle. It should be approached from the point of education, culture, and spiritual endowment. These, and these alone, make for equality—not just being born into a certain racial, cultural, or nationalistic group. That does not make equality, although it should make for an equality of opportunity.

It does not lie within our jurisdiction to decide these things humanly, but it is given to us to pray. Our prayer is not for an end to interracial strife or that the world be humanly better. It is given to us to pray that God's kingdom be realized on earth, that the activity of the Christ be made manifest in human consciousness, and that the carnal mind be recognized for the nonpower it is in the presence of the Christ. A group of earnest students praying in this way really constitutes a spiritual underground. Praying this prayer, we shall witness changes taking place on earth.

The Carnal Mind Operating in Human Relationships

Let us apply this now to our immediate families, including our aunts, uncles, nieces, and nephews. We do not have to look far to see the carnal mind operating. What shall we do about it? Shall we begin crusading? You know better than to try to change your relatives or to tell them what to do. That is not the way. The way is prayer; the way is to realize the activity of the Christ in human consciousness, to realize the nonpower of the carnal mind, and to realize that the carnal mind has no law to support it. We are not sitting in judgment as to who or what the carnal mind is: we are nullifying it by realizing that whatever degree of it is still in us, it, too, has to be nullified.

From our experience with our families, large or small, we know that the carnal mind is operating, and we know that it will continue to operate until one with God realizes the activity of the Christ in human consciousness and reveals the nonpower of the carnal mind. The work must be kept on an impersonal basis. There must be no pointing of fingers at persons or at ideologies; there must be no mental malpractice: there must be only the realization of the activity of the Christ and the nonpower of the carnal mind, and then let it be.

The carnal mind does not always act wickedly. There have been cases of men in public life who personally have not been dishonest, yet whose lives were ruined by corruption. The carnal mind had blinded them to what was going on and caused them to trust the wrong persons. Even in good men, the carnal mind operates to make them careless and trusting. Therefore, when we talk about the nonpower of the carnal mind, let us also be sure that we mean good humanhood as well as bad humanhood because both are the carnal mind in operation.

How many times are good persons responsible for making parasites of those they love! In their goodness, they want to help people until eventually these people are no longer able to help themselves. This is the carnal mind acting as human good.

What we want is the realization of the activity of the Christ in human consciousness, and so our prayer is to recognize the Christ as the only power, the only consciousness, and the carnal mind as the "arm of flesh," or nothingness. An understanding of that kind of world work will open up many ramifications of prayer.

There have been and are people on earth today who really have attained an understanding of the nature of prayer, and a great many who have passed from the visible scene are transforming consciousness by their continued dedication to prayer. This is one reason why consciousness is becoming more spiritual. Never believe that a piling up of years or a piling up of centuries has anything to do with it. To become spiritual means to come into contact with spiritual consciousness, and so it

is the dedicated consciousness of individuals who understand the nature of prayer that is transforming the world.

Everyone who engages in a world prayer activity of
a real prayer nature, the prayer of spiritual contact—not
the kind of prayer that asks God to do something, to
give him victory and his opponent defeat—must be
reaching somebody, somewhere. Someone on a sickbed
is being healed; someone on a deathbed is being raised
up; someone in an accident is being lifted up; or someone in some phase of mortality is being led to where he
is going to meet the person or the book that will set him
on the Path. So I see it as a mission of every Infinite
Way student to give not less than one period each day
for an intelligent world meditation.

"Inasmuch as Ye Have Done It"

Take what is given in this chapter as a basis, and then
let the Father reveal whatever else is necessary. The
work set forth here is merely to show the general nature
of our world work. As you work with this idea, you will
receive more specific instructions from within because
this type of prayer leads to inner communion. You are
going within for light, wisdom, and instruction, and
because it is a two-way process of communion, the
Christ comes back and gives the word to you. Sometimes it may just say, "Not by might, nor by power,"[6]
and then as you relax in the Spirit, it will be done. You
will be more deeply empowered from on High, and that
is what counts, not words.

This brings up one question: Should the persons who
are out crusading and doing human good not be doing
that? Certainly they should, because that is the highest

sense of service that they have at the moment, and some of the spiritual prayers going on here or on the other side may be raising up those very individuals who are out doing the crusading. In other words, I do not think that Florence Nightingale went out and did all she did simply because she was a good human being. I believe that the Spirit of God animated her at every step. I do not think that the leaders of the French, American, and the South American revolutions were all humanly good men. Many were under spiritual orders and could not have done otherwise.

Whether we are the spiritual power that raises up that seed or whether we are one of the seeds raised up to go out on the battlefront, we must not underestimate the value of those who are out on the front, more especially those who are out there under divine orders.

Engaging in this world work is a givingness, because it is inevitable that the Soul-center will be touched in some of your meditations and those receptive will be blessed; but remember that in that givingness is the return of your bread on the waters unto yourself, and that without your placing this bread on the water, there is no bread out there to return to you.

So it is on every level of life. Did not the Master remind us: "Inasmuch as ye have done it unto one of the least of these my brethren, ye have done it unto me"[7]; and "Inasmuch as ye did it not to one of the least of these, ye did it not to me"[8]? Remember, therefore, when you are doing this spiritual work, you are doing it unto "the least of these my brethren," and you are doing it unto the very Christ of your own being. When you are not doing it for "the least of these"—the service or the prayer—you are just withholding from yourself.

In thirty or more years of this work, I have learned that the only fruitage that comes back to me and causes me to prosper spiritually, as well as materially, is this dedication and this service to "the least of these," to the greatest of these—call it what you will. The measure of the dedication and the service of my life in the past thirty years has been the measure of my prosperity, my inner joy, and my outer experience. That is why I share it so joyously with you!

~ 8 ~

THE WAY OF GRACE

In the metaphysical world, the attention given the subject of supply is almost equal to the attention given the subject of health. Sometimes, however, spiritual freedom in the area of supply is not as easily attained as is freedom in the area of health. But because the basic truth about health is also the truth about supply, there should be no difference in attaining the consciousness of either supply or health. Nevertheless there seems to be; and often it is not easy to convince the human mind of the ever-availability of supply. A person may have been on the metaphysical path ten, twenty, or thirty years, but when the thought of supply comes to his mind, with it comes the thought of money, also, because to him supply and money are synonymous. Of course, they are not the same at all, but because they seem to be the same to the human mind, it is difficult to separate the one from the other.

Contrary to all human belief, supply is the word of God, and unless we are receiving the word of God, we are not receiving supply. "Man shall not live by bread alone, but by every word that proceedeth out of the mouth of God."[1] Bread alone does not suffice. No, we live by every word that proceeds out of the mouth of God. Daily we pray for bread, but not for baker's bread. We pray for the bread that is the word of God, and the way in which we receive it is to open our consciousness to receive that Word which is the bread of life, the meat, the wine and the water.

Anyone who believes that he is going to be fed permanently and abundantly by any other means than by receiving the word of God has entirely missed the way. No matter how much money a person might temporarily have, without the word of God he does not have supply: he merely has money, and it has been truly said that money has wings.

Receptivity to God's Grace, Essential

We do not live by money but by the grace of God, and that Grace is already within our consciousness because God constitutes our consciousness. Therefore, we are never separate or apart from our supply, but when we speak of supply, we are not speaking of money. In the whole kingdom of God, there is no money, there are no houses, and there are no automobiles. God knows nothing of food, clothing, and housing, so praying to God for such things is a waste of time. It is a form of paganism. It goes back to the ancient days when people thought of God as the source of gold and silver, and all material things. God is not the source of material things, but God is the source of the substance that appears outwardly as gold, silver, trees, and all the good of this universe.

In the kingdom of God, there is only life and love. These are the two great qualities of God: life and love—just life and love, and such additional facets as wisdom and intelligence, which are offshoots of the two great qualities, life and love. But unless we have God's love, which is the substance of all form, we will never have the form.

Therefore, when we open our consciousness to God as love, love is the substance or fulfillment of supply. It is love that puts leaves and fruit on trees; it is love that gives us divine Grace; it is the love of God that appears outwardly as what we call food, clothing, and housing. We open our consciousness to God's grace, God's love, to the substance of all form, the Spirit of God. "Where the Spirit of the Lord is, there is liberty"[2]–freedom from lack and limitation, from sin and disease. To go to God for anything but the Spirit of God is to pray amiss.

Our first act, our repeated act throughout the day, and our final act at night, therefore, is closing our eyes and opening our ears consciously to realize that the kingdom of God, the allness of God, is within us. It does not come to us because we earn it; it does not come to us because of somebody's good will; it does not even come to us because we deserve it.

God's grace is omnipresent, and not only is it omnipresent, it is infinite. But it is not available except as we specifically open our consciousness to receive it. God's grace falls alike on the just and the unjust, and we do not have to be what the world calls good to receive that Grace. As a matter of fact, very often the prodigal receives a little bit more than the humanly virtuous person. The one requirement is opening consciousness to receive It. That is the price God has placed on the infinity of supply: opening consciousness; and it is not that God put that price on it: it is that through the closing of our consciousness we have shut out God's grace. God makes no distinction between the good and the bad. God's abundance is never withheld from anyone, regardless of his sins, nor is it ever given to anyone because of his virtue. All this is a part of human superstition.

Lack and limitation and every other ill that man seems heir to come about through our failure to keep our consciousness active, alert, alive, and above all, receptive. All that is necessary, therefore, to enjoy the infinity of God's supply without limitation is to recognize that supply is not material, and then to open consciousness to receive it.

God's supply and God's grace are not received in the pocketbook: they are received in consciousness, and when they are received in our consciousness it does not take very long for them to translate themselves into the pocketbook. But we have nothing to do, at the moment, with a pocketbook: we have to do with receiving God's grace.

Our whole experience after we come into the Infinite Way should be lived from the standpoint of the truth that we are the offspring of God, that is, that we are spiritual, heirs of God and joint-heirs to all the heavenly riches. And yet, if we have been trained in metaphysics, we try to turn those heavenly riches into houses, automobiles, and dollars. But we cannot approach the subject of supply from the orthodox metaphysical idea of demonstrating effects because this attempt usually ends in failure. The fact of the matter is that students have sometimes demonstrated effects and then have been very sorry later.

"My grace is sufficient for thee"[3] does not mean that God's grace gives us dollars, automobiles, and houses. It plainly states that "My grace is sufficient." As spiritual beings, we have to be satisfied with that promise, and all we must seek is Grace.

Grace always interprets Itself at the level of the experience of the moment in which we are living. As we realize the sufficiency of God's grace, It will appear to us as air to breathe, transportation, dollars, or whatever our life may require, and It can very well appear in forms that we could not possibly expect. Our idea of what constitutes supply, of where we would like to live, or what work we would like to do may differ entirely from God's idea for us.

Let the Divine Destiny Be Revealed in Us

As offspring of God, we must remember that being His children is far different from being children of human parents. When parents have children, they do not know what purpose they have been brought to earth to fulfill. They bring them into the world, try to give them some kind of guidance, and hope for the best. But how can parents guide their children except in accord with their own concept of what is right?

In my case, my father, who was a businessman, thought that the highest right was to make a businessman of me, and yet all the time the divine plan was that I should be in religious work. Because of that, I had to fight my way out of the business world, not because my father did not love me, but because my father's idea of what was good and right for me was what was good and right for him.

But this is not true of God. God is omniscience, and when God has a child, it is for a specific purpose. There is something definite in mind with every individual offspring, something that he was actually sent into expression to do.

As human beings, we have completely missed the mark because most of the activities of human beings were not intended for us, and in our ignorance of our divine destiny, we went into something quite unrelated to that destiny.

So when we say, "Thy grace is my sufficiency in all things," we have to turn within with an open mind, and stand on that word "Grace," and let It assume the form necessary. If It shocks us out of our skins, we have to be willing to be shocked. If It makes us leave mother, father, brother, and sister, we leave mother, father, brother, and sister. If It makes us leave our homeland to go to a distant country to carry the message, we leave our homes and go where It takes us. Saul of Tarsus humanly never intended to be a carrier of the Christian message to Europe and Asia, but that is what he became the moment he came under Grace.

We have no right to outline the form Grace is to take in our experience. But if we keep ourselves open to God's gift of Grace, we can very well be more surprised at the form It takes than a child going to the Christmas tree on Christmas morning and finding the things he does not expect. What he receives is his parents' sense of love. They are giving their child, not necessarily what the child wants, but what the parents feel is for his good.

This is much more true when we go to the Father for divine Grace. It is utterly useless to have an idea of what gifts we would like, what form Grace should assume, or what form supply should take. Omniscience knows all, and It knows all about every individual because omniscience is the allness of every individual. Therefore, omniscience operates within us to reveal Its plan for us. "Nevertheless not my will, but thine, be done."[4]

God Translates Itself In Terms of Human Needs

As we take no thought for what we shall eat, what we shall drink, or wherewithal we shall be clothed, this Grace translates Itself into terms of food, clothing, housing, transportation, and all those things needful for our human experience. But if we insist on taking thought for these things, we lose our entire spiritual demonstration of peace and harmony because God knows nothing of food, clothing, housing, or transportation. God knows no more about how our ancestors transported themselves on donkeys than he does about the increasing mobility that has come to us through the use of automobiles or airplanes. God knows no more about the unleavened bread of our ancestors than he does about the overly refined nutritionless bread that we buy in our supermarkets of today.

God's grace! God feeds, clothes, houses, maintains, and sustains His image and likeness, not by any act of yours or mine, but by an act of divine Grace. Our only activity is receptivity, but we cannot stand with a begging bowl and be receptive, nor can we stand with an open pocketbook and be receptive. We must open the only thing through and as which God appears: our consciousness. God appears and acts in, and through, and as consciousness.

It is as if we were opening our ears to the realization of the truth that God's grace is our sufficiency. In such receptivity, God's grace is pouring through to us. Then all that we have to do is to be about our business, whatever it may be, taking no thought for the morrow, just doing those things which are necessary for us to do, returning half a dozen or a dozen times a day to the opening of the inner ear to God's grace, to God's supply, and then going about our business.

We have nothing to do with the way in which supply reaches us. All we have to do is to recognize that God is Spirit, and therefore supply is spiritual. We have to open our consciousness to receive it, and then, in whatever way is natural for us, the heavens open, figuratively speaking, and our supply appears. We are not to take thought as to how that is to be. We are merely to do that which is at hand for us to do, leaving the means with the Father within.

In all the miraculous ways which God has, supply always appears. It appeared to the Hebrews when they were fleeing from Egypt. It appeared: it fell right out of the sky, and let no one ever doubt that it did.

God's Grace Is Not the Prerogative of One Sex

It is true that some of us have been business men and women and have thought that our supply must come through business, and then some of us have had the joy of witnessing how we were removed from the business world, and supply still came in. Others have thought that because they were housewives their supply had to come from their husbands, only to find suddenly that they were painting, writing, or doing something else equally creative, sometimes even engaging in healing work. So they discovered that God never decreed that their support should come from, or be dependent upon, their husbands. That is just a man-made custom, and some day we are all going to be sufficiently awake to realize that each one of us derives his supply from the same God. Then, if we wish to share it voluntarily with husband or wife, we will. It never was spiritually meant that God's grace should fall only on one sex, the male. God's grace also falls on the female sex, and the day must come when it is recognized that it does so equally.

The point that I am making is that God's grace is an act of consciousness—of the male consciousness and of the female consciousness—and it is only as we, male and female, open our consciousness to that fact that we discover the spiritual source of supply and realize that there is just as much of it in the female consciousness as in the male, with or without the help of the other.

That does not mean that each one must earn a separate livelihood. It means that each one is going to realize that as he or she receives Grace from God, he or she will contribute to the other, probably one in one form and one in another.

Witness that in our modern world more women are working and earning money than ever before. But this is really only a prelude to a great experience that is coming when neither male nor female will have to struggle for a living. Evidently that day can be ushered in only when it has been proved to the women of the world that they have as much access to supply as the men have, and that God's grace is a universal and an equal experience.

As we are receptive to the grace of God, It will appear as supply. More and more the truth will be revealed that one sex is not dependent on another for supply, but that both sexes are dependent on the kingdom of God that is established within them. Then they can share with one another, and that day will come.

So let us never forget that when we open our ears and minds in receptivity, we are not going to God for material supply—for money, automobiles, houses, or clothing: we are realizing that God's grace is "closer. . . than breathing, and nearer than hands and feet."[5] The ears are open to hear; the mind is open to receive; and what we receive is the Spirit of God, the awareness and the feeling of the Presence. This is God's supply. When we receive This, It, in a way unknown to us, is translated in our human picture as food, clothing, housing, money, or whatever form it is that the supply must take.

The reason that the world as a whole does not receive God's supply is that it is turning to God for those material things of which God has no awareness, when the truth is that it is legitimate to turn to God only for His Grace, His love, His peace, and to know His will. God is Spirit, and to go to God for anything but spiritual awareness is like going to a pauper for money, like going to somebody for something that he does not have.

God does not have money. God does not have gold, silver, or diamonds. God does not have meat, potatoes, fish, or vegetables. God knows nothing of those things. All that God knows is the Spirit which, through God's grace, is upon us. We translate This into food, clothing, and housing in terms of our particular conditioning. For example, two thousand years ago donkeys were considered an adequate form of transportation; today we are satisfied with nothing less than jet planes flying a thousand miles an hour, and upwards.

Prayer, an Opening of Consciousness

Prayer is effective only in the measure that we go to God without a desire because otherwise we are holding a mold up to God and arbitrarily saying, "Fill it for me.

Here is the mold of my wish, of my desire. Become my servant and do what I would like." The Infinite Way knows no such form of prayer.

We cannot ask God for anything. If we did, we would be dishonoring God. We would virtually be saying, "God, I know what I need, but you do not, so I will tell you." Remember, we are saying this to the infinite Intelligence that created the whole universe, including us. How stupid it must seem—not to God, because He would not know how stupid we can be. But think how stupid it is to plead, "Give me food," and "Give me clothing," and "Give me housing."

It is the same in our healing work. There is no use in going to God with the desire that God heal us of our diseases or that God heal this inharmony or that lack. Real prayer is an opening of consciousness to God, and then a communing within.

The fruitage of this kind of prayer is that sooner or later the revelation is given to us from within, "Do not look to *Me* because you are ever with *Me,* and all that *I* have is already yours. It was incorporated in you in the beginning, 'before Abraham was.'[6] "

Teaching Givingness

In the beginning, because of our oneness with God, He incorporated into us His life, His mind, His soul, His Spirit, His substance, His supply, and His infinity. He can add nothing to us now, nor are there any powers on earth to take anything from us as long as we live in the realization that infinity, Grace, and the gift of God are ours by virtue of our relationship to God, that oneness that was established within in the beginning. When this is revealed to us and perceived by us, we can understand why we must open out a way for "the imprisoned splendour"[7] to escape. Since infinity is the measure of our supply and since nothing can be added to it, we must begin to pour; we must start the outflow.

In every department of life, we must constantly search, not to see how we can get something, or what we can get, but in what way we can pour. The damming up of supply results from our failure to pour in some manner.

There are times when we may find it difficult to impart this to students because an embarrassment arises. Some students may get the impression that we want them to give something to us and that we are using this gentle way of hinting. But when they are further enlightened, they will know that a teacher must already have reached that stage where he understands that he is spiritually fed and has gone beyond the point of looking to students or patients for his supply.

No thought of gain ever enters the spiritual teacher's consciousness, because the spiritual teacher does not go into this kind of a ministry until he has demonstrated that he is living by God's grace. Then, when he has demonstrated that, he can freely teach that the secret of supply is in giving, in pouring.

We are not concerning ourselves at the moment merely with money, although sharing in this concrete way is a kind of givingness that cannot be ignored. However, important as this form of sharing is, money is the least of the pouring and the givingness of which we are talking. The real givingness is the sharing of the spiritual treasures that have been given so freely and so abundantly to us. The kingdom of God is full of spiritual treasures, and since that Kingdom is within us, we are a storehouse of spiritual riches, but we are not a storehouse in the sense of withholding them: we are storing up these treasures by distributing or sharing them, because it is only in the spending of them that we really store them up.

To the human sense this is, of course, a contradiction, but anyone who has ever had any teaching experience must know that the more he teaches a subject, whether he is teaching bookkeeping, architecture, language, science, or art, the greater knowledge and understanding of it he himself has. The more he imparts, the greater is his own unfoldment.

God's Grace, the Gift of Himself

God's grace is the gift of Himself appearing on earth as us. God, the Father, is appearing on earth as God, the son; and these are one, not two. Therefore, all that the Father has is ours; all that God is, we are, once we have overcome our religious superstition and ignorance.

"He that seeth me seeth him that sent me[8] . . . [for] I and my Father are one."[9] There is lack and limitation in the world because the people of the world have forgotten this. They have set themselves apart as if there were a God up there and they were down here. They believe that God has lost sight of them, and through their many petitions, they are trying to remind God that they are down here in lack, forgetting that the kingdom of God is within them, not up there, and that God is omniscience, the all-knowing.

In trying to tell God anything regarding your needs or my needs or the world's needs, how clear it is that if

God could be insulted, we would be insulting Deity. Fortunately, just as a little child cannot insult its parents because the parents understand the child's ignorance, so God cannot be insulted by us. God is Spirit; we are spiritual; our needs are spiritual; our supply is spiritual; and because of our oneness with God, it is all omnipresent where we are. If we were separated from God, we might have to do something about it; but all we have to do is to recognize:

"I and my Father are one," and where the kingdom of God is, I am, for we are one.

Then we turn within in that oneness, not for money, not for food, not for clothing, not for housing, but for His grace:

Thy grace is my sufficiency; the will of God is my sufficiency; the love of God is my sufficiency.

God's Grace Is Dependent on the Awareness of Our Relationship of Oneness with Him

Within ourselves, we are receptive, not to money: to love. We are receptive to the love of God that is within us; we are receptive to the grace of God that is always upon us. In our stillness, we develop a sense of receptivity: the ears are open, the mind is awake, and we are receiving. What are we receiving? The grace of God which is the word of God and which is spiritual. Then we go about our business. If we are in the wrong business, it will not be long before we will be moved into the right business.

Years ago, a man who came to me for help had just such an experience. He was working for a brewery, doing window dressing of signs in beer saloons and, as part of his work, buying beer for whoever was in the place. This man was ill, and he had tried to get spiritual help from several metaphysicians, but they would not give it to him because he was working for a brewery, and that was the wrong business. Eventually he was sent to me. I told him that he did not have to give up his position and that God's grace was not dependent on something he did or did not do, but that God's grace was dependent on what he was, an offspring of God. That is the only qualification for receiving God's good.

It makes no difference if a person is dressing windows in a saloon or if he is the thief on the cross. It has nothing to do with God. God's grace is dependent on a person's relationship to Him, and that relationship is oneness. The truth of "I and my Father are one" stands whether we are saints or sinners, whether we are good or evil. Our relationship to God cannot be changed; and in any instant in which we realize our divine sonship, God's grace is upon us.

This Grace will take care of our supply and our health. It will even change our natures. But if God's grace were dependent on our first being virtuous, I am afraid that none of us would make the grade. If God's grace were dependent on our being good first, we would still be outside the kingdom of heaven begging; but it is not that way at all, I can assure you.

The adulteress, the thief on the cross, the syphilitic, all received God's grace. When? In the moment that they opened themselves to it, not by being reformed first. No, there are many things we ourselves cannot really do much about, and unless we receive the grace of God we are not going to be reformed. There are things that are wrong with many of us that none of the ministers and none of the doctors can cure, so if God is going to withhold His grace until those things are healed, it is going to be too late for most of us.

The truth is that God's grace falls on the saint and the sinner alike, the minute an individual opens himself to that Grace. We must open ourselves to God in our sins as well as in our saintliness, and discover that it is by opening consciousness to God's grace that the sins and the desire for sin disappear. Trying to be good before we go to God is putting the cart before the horse. Let us go to God before we are good and find that this going to God provides the goodness.

Let us forget for a moment that we are male or female; let us forget that we are saint or sinner; let us forget that we have or have not arrived at some degree of spirituality. Let us forget all that, and let us just be receptive to divine Grace.

Thy grace, omnipresent, is my sufficiency in sickness and in health. Thy grace is my sufficiency whether or not I humanly deserve it. Spiritually, I am the child of God, and God has never disinherited any of His children, whatever their human faults.

Regardless of what we humanly may be or may have been, in that moment when we open our consciousness to the nature of the Divine, though our sins were scarlet, we are white as snow. It does not make any difference if those sins continue to persist for a while because sometimes just the tenacity of habit makes them continue in effect, even after they have inwardly been forsaken. But pay no attention to that; ignore that.

Only one thing matters. From the moment that our consciousness is opened to receive an inner Grace, our sins begin to be dissolved. With some persons, it is an instantaneous process; in some, the faults and sins drag on a while. But from the time that we wholeheartedly turn in a spiritual direction, these sins are dissolved, the penalties for them begin to disappear, and we are on the way to living under Grace.

Outwardly, nothing may seem to happen, and in other cases, something very dramatic happens, and sometimes we are more puzzled about that because we do not know what it is that has happened. The point is that we live by Grace, and in the moment that we recognize this and abide in this truth, we live "not by might, nor by power."[10] We do not then live by our brains or by our virtues: we live by divine Grace.

From that moment on, the new way opens, not always as quickly as we would like; not even all of our bad traits disappear as quickly as we would hope for, nor our lacks and limitations. But be assured that from the moment we have recognized our oneness with the Father, the sins, the sinful thoughts, the false appetites, and the bad habits begin to disappear, and we are living a life by Grace.

~9~

Beyond the Pairs of Opposites to Being

Infinity exists within ourselves, the infinity of any and every form that may ever be necessary to our experience. Whether that form is to appear outwardly as words, thoughts, or ideas; whether it is to appear outwardly as designs in clothing, architecture, or bridges, regardless of what form we are to bring forth on earth, its abiding place is within our consciousness. Every word of the Infinite Way message, therefore, is meant to drive us back into our consciousness to draw forth the infinity of supply that is there.

Supply of every nature is as infinite and inexhaustible as the words and messages that have come out of my mouth these past years. It is new and fresh every day if we do not depend on yesterday's manna but develop the habit of going within to our consciousness to draw forth fresh supply. It is only in proportion as we think of yesterday's supply as being today's supply that we sometimes run into lack; but as we learn to turn within for a fresh supply we draw forth God's grace in new forms, bigger forms, richer forms.

For seventeen years, the message that has found its way into the Infinite Way writings kept pouring through, and if it had not been the word of God, it would have been so stale and monotonous that no one would have read it. But supply is infinite; and therefore it is always fresh and new when it comes forth from the grace of God and not out of the stored-up memory of an individual.

In spiritual truth, we do not depend on what we knew yesterday, nor do we even want to live on the money we had yesterday. We do not waste it, I do not mean that; but each day must be a new day in which we go within for God's grace, and we can have no idea what form God's grace is going to take. That, too, is our good fortune because that opens out the way for the new forms, the greater forms, and the greater wisdoms that are to unfold from within our consciousness.

Grace Appears as Form

Again I must remind you that turning within can only be for Grace because the moment we think of forms of architecture, amounts of money, or plots for plays, we have lost it. The kingdom of God has none of those things. The only thing that the kingdom of God has is Grace, and as we turn within for Grace, that Grace will appear as the form necessary to our experience.

The only way I can describe it is by remembering my childhood and recalling how my mother would whip up a great big dish of dough, and then when she pressed the dough into different kinds of little tins it came out in the shape of fish, elephants, or birds. We could have as many forms as we had tins, but it was the same dough *appearing* as those different forms.

We cannot go to God for forms: we cannot ask God to design a house for us, to heal a disease, or to sell our apple pies. We go to God for Grace. This is the substance. If a person is an architect, Grace will appear as the new forms he needs; if he is an artist or a designer, Grace will appear as the skill and the designs; if he is a metaphysician, Grace will appear as healing. Whatever any one of us may need, Grace appears as that form. But for us to go to God to learn how to make apple pies would be a failure because it is not God who knows anything about apple pies or how to make them: it is God's grace that reveals to us how to make apple pies if that happens to be our need.

When you turn within, turn within for Grace. It makes no difference whether you need health, wealth, or ideas, you go to God only for Grace, and that Grace appears outwardly as the form necessary to your experience. Therefore, if your need today is food, It comes forth as food; if it is transportation, It comes forth as transportation; if it is an idea, It will come forth as an idea. But always remember this, God knows nothing of the forms: God knows only Grace.

God knows nothing of health because God knows nothing of the lack of health; therefore, there is no use in going to God for health. But God knows nothing of the opposite of health, either. In God there is neither health nor illness: there is only the perfection of God's being. Very often students lose the way because they are seeking something through God of which God has no awareness.

When you go within, you go within for a realization of God's grace, and God's grace appears to you as health, but God's grace appears to another person as a new design, whether for a bridge, a house, a dress, a new kind of food, or a new type of transportation. And yet God knows nothing of those things.

God has no knowledge of health; God has no knowledge of wealth. God is Spirit, and the kingdom of God is spiritual. Therefore, when you go to God, you can go only for Grace. God's grace is your sufficiency in all things, whether it is a sufficiency of health, supply, or talent.

Goodness and Badness, Human Evaluations

Regardless of your present human status, whether you are saint or sinner, I am sure that God is unaware of it. God's awareness extends only to a knowledge of His own nature, and there is nothing saintly and nothing "sinnerly" about God. God is infinite being. To be a saint, He would have to be something better than something else, and in God there is no better and there is no worse: there is only One.

So it is with us! If, by some kind of accidental chance, you are and always have been good, forget it as fast as you can because it may keep you out of the kingdom of heaven. I do not believe that there is any more room in heaven for good people than for bad people. Whether to human sense you appear to be good-being at the moment or bad-being, as a human being you have potentialities either way, and anything could come along and upset the balance. Therefore, forget goodness and badness, and just remember being. Forget about your humanhood, and remember that in your divine being all that God is, you are, and all that the Father has is yours. Then open your ears inwardly to be receptive.

When the word of God comes to you, you will discover that you will lose your sense of goodness and your sense of badness. You will have no more awareness of being good than you have of being bad. All you will remember is that you are being, and as a matter of fact, *you* are really not being: God is being you. There will then be no possibility of your sitting in judgment on your fellow man who may be bad only out of ignorance or who may be good out of stupidity. There are countless stupid good people, and there are countless good people who are good merely because they are afraid to be bad.

Put aside all this business about goodness and badness and be spiritual. Be of the household of God: neither good nor bad, just spiritual. Then, as you develop this inner capacity to listen, your actions are guided by God, and they are neither good nor bad: they are just whatever it is that God meant them to be.

You, yourself, have no way of judging your actions because anything that you call "good" is merely your human evaluation of it. But, by observing your reactions, a person can almost determine what kind of a home you came from and what its standards of good and evil were. They may have been entirely different from those of another family, which also had standards of good and evil that may or may not have been actually good or evil.

Both Goodness and Badness Must Give Way to Being

In the Infinite Way, you never judge as to whether you are good or whether you are bad because unless you are willing to lose both your goodness and your badness you are not going to arrive at the kingdom of God. Be assured that there is no clinging to goodness in the kingdom of God: there is only Being.

But think what happens once you recognize that there is only one Being. That means that your being is my being, and therefore you cannot be good to me or bad to me: you can be to me only what you are to yourself. That is all!

God does not bestow His grace in different degrees on His children because the truth is that God has only one child, one offspring, one life. No matter how many billion times it may be lived on earth, it is the one life that is being lived. Therefore, God is the same to all. It does not look that way, but the degree of harmony in your experience represents the degree in which you know this truth. That is what determines your life experience.

Once you come to the realization of God as your life, then and only then can you realize that both the goodness and the badness of your human life have to be overcome in order that you can ultimately say, "Why callest thou me good? there is none good but one, that is, God."[1] That is the good that is flowing; that is the good that is healing; that is the good that is enriching; that is the good that is forgiving—not you, not I, but that which flows from the Father as the son.

Only in your surrender of the belief in your goodness as well as your badness, can you attain spiritually. As long as you persist in remembering the evil that has found an outlet through you, just so long will you keep yourself out of the kingdom of heaven. But, too, just as long as you keep remembering the good that has been expressed through you, just so long, also, will you keep yourself out of the kingdom of heaven.

When you begin to realize that evil, as such, has been a part of your existence only through ignorance, and goodness has been a part of your existence only by the grace of God, you come to that place where you become an absolute instrument for the grace of God to flow. You become a blessing, not only to yourself, but to everyone who comes within range of your experience.

How many hundreds of persons have come to the Infinite Way in lack and found abundance, have come in sin and found holiness! Ask yourself why. Have all these persons become saints? No, humanly, none of us ever will be completely a saint or a sinner, but regardless of what degree of either of these we may have been, it must be overcome until we come to the recognition that neither our human good nor our human bad is the ultimate determination of how far we have gone on the spiritual path. The ultimate determination is the recognition of our spiritual identity.

The records of the past show some sinners who have become saints, some dead who have become alive, and some poor who have become rich. Why? By the recognition that the whole kingdom of God is within. It makes no difference at this moment whether that "you" is a saint or a sinner: the kingdom of God is within, and in the moment that you begin to give recognition to this, and even while your sins are continuing, that recognition will be the purifying experience. Then you will soon see what happens in the realm of supply.

Supply, an Activity of Consciousness, Not a Reward for Goodness

In the area of supply, there is lack and abundance only as long as you are dealing in the human realm. There is neither lack nor abundance in the spiritual realm, despite the fact that some persons believe that there is. They believe that the kingdom of God is just overflowing with gold, silver, diamonds, and other priceless things; but I am sure that when you get to heaven you will find that there is not a scrap of anything stored up there at all because all heaven is, is consciousness unfolding, and it unfolds as the need appears.

Supply does not come because you are good, and lack does not come because you are bad. You can be bad and have supply, and you can be good and have no supply, and vice versa. Lack comes because of the belief that supply is something tangible, and most of us are not only struggling for it, but laying it up where moth and rust corrupt.

Supply is omnipresent, and it has nothing to do with saintliness or sinfulness. Supply is omnipresent! When you recognize that, the miracle takes place. The sinner, without even thinking of wanting to be a saint, becomes one. Persons have been held in bondage to sin by believing they were going to get everything they desired when they became good, and they have tried to become good. But even with that incentive, they could not become good, and even if they did, they did not get the supply, and therefore many of them went back to being bad.

Whether you are a saint or a sinner, you and your Father are one, and all that the Father has is yours. Although you may not experience it while you are a sinner, nevertheless it is true. If you know this truth when you are a sinner, it will make you a saint. Why? Most of the evil in the world comes about because persons are trying to get something they do not have and want, but that striving automatically disappears when they have everything that they possibly can want all the time, without even trying for it.

Become an Instrument as Which God
Is Living on Earth

All that the Father has is yours. What does the Father have? Life, love! These are the two great facets of the Father: life and love. And the life of the Father is your life; the love of the Father is your love. You come into the demonstration of this by your inner attunement, by your recognition of the truth of oneness, and then by letting the flow take place—not by trying to change your outer conduct.

If you are sinning in some way, it may be that you will keep on until the sin stops. If you are being good, you may keep on being good until that, too, stops, because be assured of this, being good has to stop, the same as being bad. Until you stop being either good or bad, you are not going to show forth the kingdom of God or the son of God which you are. Goodness and badness are illusions brought on by a human sense of what constitutes good and bad. Both goodness and badness have to come to an end until you are neither good nor bad: you are just the instrument as which God is living on earth.

Now we come to as important a place as you will ever come to in the spiritual life, and that is to the point where you face yourself with the truth that you are neither good nor evil. The evil that you have done is due to the ignorance into which you were born; the good that you think you have done stems from the religious training and home environment into which you were born. But you, yourself, can be neither good nor evil.

You are of the household of God, and the qualities and the activities of God are yours. They are not yours *per se:* they are yours by the grace of God, they are God's qualities manifest as you. You cannot take pride in your goodness; you cannot take pride in your virtues; you cannot take pride in your health. All you can do is to recognize that the grace of God is upon you. Health is the grace of God; supply is the grace of God; purity is the grace of God.

When you come to this state of consciousness, you will understand that life is lived by Grace, and you will have dropped your human qualities of goodness and your human qualities of badness. Any belief in your goodness is as evil as the belief in your badness, just as the belief in your prosperity is as evil as the belief in lack because prosperity is no more yours than lack. Prosperity is the gift of God, and there is no lack to those who know that. Lack is the product of the belief that supply is mine, yours, his, or hers. This is where lack comes from: the belief that somebody has supply.

When we come to this subject of good and evil, lack and abundance, purity and sinfulness, or spirituality and materiality, we perpetuate the entire human experience by the belief that we are good or evil, that we are sick or well, that we are rich or poor. We come into and under the grace of God only in the realization that we are living by God's grace.

If you have what the world calls virtue or goodness, it is yours by the grace of God. If you have what is called abundance, it is by the grace of God. If you have health, it is by the grace of God. In the realization of this you surrender the false sense of human health, human supply, human sinfulness. You surrender all that, and then you begin to live under and by the grace of God, but not until you have lost all sense of being either good or bad, rich or poor, abundant or lacking, saint or sinner, and have realized that the life you live is lived by the grace of God.

Then you will discover that you have lost the pairs of opposites, and you will find yourself just living. You will not even be living: God will be living Itself, and you will always be living with an attentive ear, watching the life of God unfold within your own self.

Living, Not Preaching, Attracts

At the present time, fortunately, we have a sense of balance that enables us to live in "this world"[2] but not be of it, that makes it possible to live with our fellow man without seeming to be "crackpots." This sense of balance keeps this truth locked up within ourselves and prevents us from giving it to others except as they come seeking it, hungering and thirsting for it, and then feeding it to them only in small doses until we are assured that they can eat the "meat" of the Word. The mistake too many persons in the religious world have made is setting themselves apart from others, whereas, the setting apart should be only within themselves.

Outwardly, live as other men. Inwardly, live by Grace, and thereby attract to yourself those ready for the Word. Do not preach it, because you will drive them away with your preachments. Do not try to appear different from other men; do not wear halos; do not use a language that sets you apart and makes others think, "Oh, you must be some kind of a saint." Do not do that! If you attain any degree of saintliness, keep it hidden within, and appear outwardly to the world as other men, yet not acting as other men: acting from within, from the saintliness that has developed within.

No one is ever going to be attracted to a spiritual message by hearing someone preach it, because preaching reaches only as far as the human mind. Living it reaches the Soul, and that is why all the preaching there has been for six thousand years has not changed men. They are still out dropping bombs on one another; they are still out lying, cheating, and defrauding, in spite of all the preaching.

There must be an end to preaching; there must be an end to telling other men how to live. There must come an understanding of the nature of God as individual identity, locking that understanding up within ourselves, letting it shine out, and then feeding it slowly and gradually to those who seek it. It is not accomplished by appearing to be different from other men, but by *being different,* different only to the degree of the spiritual awareness that has unfolded within us, and not trying to be better than what we have realized or trying to use the language of truth when we have not attained the consciousness of it.

Evil, Spiritual Ignorance

The day comes when you will realize, not only that you are not evil, but that you never have been evil, regardless of what evil sense may have had possession of you at some time through spiritual ignorance. Then, too, you will realize that you are not good and never have been good. Any qualities of good to which you have given expression have been that degree of godliness that has expressed itself through you.

When you realize, "I have never been evil, and I have never been good. The evil that manifested itself through me was due to an ignorance of truth, and the good that manifested itself through me was my good fortune in having the grace of God shine through, not through any personal virtue of mine," then, in that degree do you come to this place where you will definitely know that you cannot be a saint or a sinner, that you cannot be rich or poor, that you cannot be sick or well.

You can be none of those things because the grace of God is your life. It never changes, and It is no different in one than in another:

It is the grace of God that lives my life, and I am neither good nor bad; I am neither rich nor poor; I am neither saint nor sinner; I am neither sick nor well; I am neither alive nor dead. I am I, and all that I AM is, I am.

I am neither Jew nor Gentile; I am neither white, black, nor yellow. I am I! All that God is, I am; all that the Father has is mine.

"I" Is the Word

Live in the inner awareness of *I*, of *I*-ness, *I*. *I* is the Father within you, and *I* is the son that appears outwardly. All that the Father within you is, the son without is. As long as you can live in that consciousness, you will never be good and you will never be bad; you will never be rich and you will never be poor. You will never be a saint and you will never be a sinner. You will always be *I*, and you will always be showing forth the *I*-ness which is God appearing as the son. You will claim no qualities for yourself: neither good nor bad, neither rich nor poor, neither saint nor sinner, neither white nor black, none of these things! You are *I!*

That word *I* is the secret of it all. Everything that the Infinite Way reveals must ultimately lead to that revelation. Say "*I*" to yourself and you will discover that *I* is neither Oriental nor Occidental. It is neither Jew nor Greek, neither bond nor free. *I* is *I.* All that God is, you are—the *I* of you—and all that the Father has is showing itself forth through you. In order to show this forth continuously on earth, the only thing you need is the willingness to share it. The moment you fail to do that, you dam it up and lose it.

Only while you are willing to share it does the flow continue, but do not share it by going out and shouting it from the housetops. Do not share it by telling it to those who are not interested. That is not sharing it: that is trying to force it on somebody. My willingness to share it is shown forth in my willingness to impart to those who seek. Come without money and come with money; come in saintliness and come in sinfulness; come any way you like, but come and receive.

There will be no praise for your goodness, and there will be no condemnation for your badness: there will be only the recognition of the saintliness which is the state of your Soul as it is, as it always will be. When you can face this world looking at everyone, seeing the saintliness of his Soul, with no judgment as to his human evil or human good, you have entered the Christ-ministry, and you are about your Father's business, *and not until then.*

~ 10 ~

INCORPOREALITY:
GOD, MAN, AND UNIVERSE

A person can rise to mystical consciousness only by the straight and narrow path, a path which has been known to every mystic throughout all the ages. It has been taught so many times that by now you might think we would all be established in the mystical consciousness.

The truth is that the interest of the world has never yet been in attaining mystical consciousness, but only in attaining the fruits of it, what the Master called "the loaves and fishes." The world has always wanted peace, but not that which will produce peace. The world has always wanted prosperity, but not that which produces prosperity. That it wants to avoid. It wants health, but not that which will produce health.

The world has been taught to pray, not for what would give peace, prosperity, and health, but for the peace, prosperity, and health themselves. There is no way to attain these through prayer. Every prayer, therefore, whether it has been a Hebrew prayer, a Christian, Hindu, Vedantic, or any other kind of prayer, has failed because it has been directed toward getting "loaves and fishes," the "things," instead of that which produces the things.

Attain the Fabric, and the Form Follows

All creation comes forth from a *source*, and if you have the source you can have the creation. But there is no way to get the creation separate and apart from the source of the creation. It is as if you set your mind on having a desk, and someone said to you, "But you must have a piece of wood before you can make a desk."

"Oh, do not bother me with that; do not bother me with that! I want a desk."

"I know, but—"

"I want a desk."

"But there is no such thing as a desk until you have the wood!"

So, if you want a desk, you will have to go and get yourself a great big tree and then you can have, not only the desk, but you can have a chair, too, and you can have shelves. In other words, you must have the wood before you can have a desk, but just as many persons try to get themselves a desk without getting the wood, so they go from one teaching to another and one church to another, always seeking health, supply, happiness, contentment, and peace. Their attitude is, "Do not waste my time with the fabric of which these are made."

The fabric of life is consciousness, spiritual consciousness, and if you want the forms of life you must have its fabric first: the consciousness. Once you have the consciousness, you can have all the things added.

This has always been known, and in every age there has been someone who has taught it. Jesus taught it in the Sermon on the Mount when he said, "Take no thought for your life, what ye shall eat, or what ye shall drink; nor yet for your body, what ye shall put on. . . . But seek ye

first the kingdom of God, and his righteousness."¹ Seek
the inner realm, consciousness, and the things will be
added unto you.

Long ago the purity of that teaching was dropped,
and instead today the prayer is: "Give me rent"; "Give
me peace"; "Give me health." People all over the world
are praying for every conceivable thing except the one
thing that the great Master told them to pray for: the
kingdom of God, Consciousness.

Incorporeal God Can Create Only Incorporeal Man

In the twelfth century, Maimonides, a great Hebrew
philosopher, emphasized the incorporeal nature of God.
In the introduction to a translation of a book by
Maimonides, *The Guide of the Perplexed*,² Leo Strauss
points up this principle in words which you are going to
find very familiar, because in them is found the essence
of the Infinite Way, even though his words came to me
only this week³:

> The chief reason why it is so urgent to establish the
> belief in God's incorporeality, however, is supplied by
> the fact that that belief is destructive of idolatry. It was
> of course universally known that idolatry is a very grave
> sin, nay, that the Law has, so to speak, no other purpose
> than to destroy idolatry. But this evil can be completely
> eradicated only if everyone is brought to know that God
> has no visible shape whatever or that He is incorporeal.
> Only if God is incorporeal is it absurd to make images
> of God and to worship such images. Only under this
> condition can it become manifest to everyone that the
> only image of God is man, living and thinking man, and
> that man acts as the image of God only through wor-
> shiping the invisible or hidden God alone.

Do you see why metaphysicians have difficulty in doing healing work? Although they, of course, recognize the incorporeality of God, they do not recognize the incorporeality of man, and consequently they deal with a structural man who has bones, a brain, liver, heart, and lungs. Consciously or unconsciously, then, when they give a treatment they are hoping to bring down the fever, remove the lump, or set the bone, and thereby they are blocking the entire treatment. They are setting up a barrier between God and man because incorporeal God cannot give birth to a corporeal man, only to incorporeal man.

Incorporeal man has no physical structure, and therefore in their meditation, prayer, and treatment, those on the mystical path must remove from thought the image-man, the corporeal man, the man who has physicality because that man is not the man of God's creating. For this reason, prayer, which really is a communion between God and man, that is, the union of God and man, can never take place between incorporeal God and corporeal man.

The moment you go to God with the idea of attaining a *thing,* the moment you go to God with something of a physical nature in thought—I do not care whether it is supply, companionship, or a new lung—you separate yourself from God, and you are maintaining that same state of separation for your patient or your student.

If I look out at a group of persons with my eyes, I can be aware only of corporeal man. That "natural" part of me, the five physical senses, can be aware only of the five physical senses of you. If I am limited to that consciousness, however, I have no right to be a meta-physical practitioner or teacher, and I have no right to claim to have attained any degree of the mystical consciousness.

Evolving Stages of Consciousness

It is true that there is a physical being, a body; and it is true that there are those persons who live completely on the physical level of life. They earn their living by their physical strength; they get their pleasures in and through the body; and their pain comes in and through the body.

Then there are those who have gone much further than that, and they have become the mental as well as the physical man: they now have a mental awareness. They not only know the physical aspects of life, but they know the mental: they know beauty; they know benevolence; and they know joy. They have a capacity for culture, refinement, education, art, literature, and science, but even then they are not the whole man, because just as man has not only a physical sense of being and a mental sense, he has within himself, also, a spiritual sense, the Christ. It is hidden from view; It has never been awakened. But It is not asleep in a person: he is asleep to It.

The Christ is never asleep in us! The Christ of us is always on Its job and awake. It is we who are asleep to It. It is there, but we are unaware of It. Throughout my lifetime I had an innate capacity to understand all the wisdom that now is in my personal library, but up to a certain age I had no access to it, and all of it was hidden from me because I had no awareness of it. Then, at a certain period of my life, I became aware of books which have recorded the wisdom of the ages, and from then on an understanding and appreciation of them were developed and brought into expression.

Similarly, throughout my life, I must have had a spiritual healing consciousness, but I did not know it. I was just as materially minded and lived as materialistically as anybody else because I knew nothing about this *thing* that was somewhere. Then, on a certain day, It burst forth, and the next day I was doing healing work.

The point is that each of us is in part a physical being; each of us is a mental being; and each of us is an incorporeal, spiritual being, and the reality of us is that incorporeal, spiritual Selfhood which is born of God. The other part of us is that creation described in the second and third chapters of Genesis, which was made, not by God, but by mind, by the mind of man, by what is called the Lord God.

God Reveals Itself in a Moment of Unknowing

If I am to acknowledge God, therefore, I must acknowledge incorporeal God, and that means not only that I cannot embrace God in a figure or form, but I cannot even embrace It in a mental image. I dare not even name It because if I call It "Spirit" or "mind," I have made an image of what I think God is. Even if I call It "love," I have made an image. All the synonyms in common use for God are just so many words. Not one of them will heal even a headache. Why? They are mental concepts: they are not God.

The only way in which I can know God is by knowing that I cannot know God, that God cannot be embraced in my mind, that God *is*. Once you acknowledge that God *is,* you are inferentially declaring that God is infinity, God is omniscience, God is omnipotence, God is omnipresence. But how can you ever know what the word "omniscience" means? How can you ever embrace in your mind what omnipotence and omnipresence mean? You cannot! Therefore, release all concepts; let them go. Do not try to understand God. Do not try to embrace God in your mind.

How, then, are you to know God aright? Ah, that you can do. You can know God. God *is.* Then *let* God define itself. All of a sudden, as you are busy *not knowing,* you are aware that something is saying to you, *"I* am God," and you look around and wonder who said it, and where It is. You will think that It is in your chest. Ah, no! The next minute you will turn around and say, "No, no! It was right over my left shoulder." Just about that time It fools you because It talks up to you from down on the floor. Then you will let go: "Aha! *I* cannot be confined inside of me or outside of me." It is neither inside nor outside because, to God, how can there be an inside and an outside? Inside of what and outside of what? There would have to be something greater than God to encompass It.

So you come to the realization that in the final analysis you cannot know God with the mind, but God can announce Itself to you. God can say, "I will never leave thee, nor forsake thee."[4] God can whisper, "*I* was with thee before Abraham was." God can assure you, "*I* will be with thee to the end of the world."

All you will ever know about God is the word *I.* That word *I* keeps repeating itself over and over and over again: "Fear not: for I am with thee."[5] You cannot see *I;* you cannot hear *I*; you cannot taste *I;* you cannot touch *I.* You cannot draw pictures of *I;* you cannot even visualize what *I* am like. *I* can never be a graven image.

The Omnipresence of "I"

When you have reached that state of consciousness, you are ready for the mystical life. When you realize that "I and my Father are one,"[6] you will know that *I* also am incorporeal and infinite. Moreover, you will know that all that God is, *I* am. This is the reason it has been possible to write or cable me from any part of the world and be healed before the message reached me. I have recognized my incorporeality; I have recognized that *I* am not in a body: *I* am speaking through the body, but *I* am not in the body.

I am where you are, and it makes no difference whether it is any place between Cape Town and London; it makes no difference whether it is anywhere between Detroit and the southern end of South America. Wherever it is, that is where *I* am because "I and my Father are one," not two. Wherever God is, *I* am; and whatever the nature of God is, is the nature of my being. Therefore, without taking thought and without directing thought, anyone who makes contact with that Spirit which *I* am has made contact with his *source*. Eventually he is going to learn that he made contact with himself because the *I* that I am is the *You* that you are.

"I" Incarnate in Many Forms

In one of my deeper meditations, when I was in full awareness of the incorporeality of my Self, I saw that *I* could incarnate as a male or a female. That is because *I*, God, is neither male nor female. There is only one *I*. Therefore, it would make no difference at all whether in another incarnation *I* appeared as a male or a female, and this will explain something else to you.

You have never had a beginning. You cannot coexist with God and have a beginning or an ending. You have always lived, and you have always lived somewhere, but you may not have lived in the part of the world where you are now living.

When you attain the incorporeal sense of your being, you will discover and know that if you existed in Europe, you were most likely white-skinned; if you existed in Africa, you were probably black-skinned; if you existed in India, you were copper-colored; if in Arabia or in the Holy Land in the time of Jesus, you were of dark complexion, or if you existed in China or Japan, you had Mongolian features. You say, "I?" Surely, yes, *I,* who else but *I?* Is there any but *I,* and has there ever been a time when *I* was not manifest? Was there ever an unmanifested *I?* Therefore, *I* has always been.

So it is, that should there be life on other planets, which I feel there must be, we have no way of knowing what the form of that life is, but be assured, *I* am incorporeal, and *I* am on those other planets. Should we in some future time manifest there, we are going to manifest in the form of life suitable to that environment, which would be nothing at all like we look now. Once you recognize the incorporeal nature of your being, you will understand why it could be taught, "There is neither Jew nor Greek."[7] And you will know why there is neither black nor white; there is neither copper nor red, neither Oriental nor Occidental. Those are merely the forms *I* assumes in order to fit into Its surroundings.

There is a time when the caterpillar is a caterpillar and has the body of a worm, and there is the time when the caterpillar becomes a butterfly and has the body of a butterfly, but it is the same life, only a different form.

The Phoenix lives as form and then becomes dust, and then lives again: nevertheless it is the same life when it is dust, the same life when it is ashes. Otherwise it could not have formed again.

"I" Speaks and "I" Hears

Do you understand the point to which I am leading? You will never do good spiritual healing work until you attain the inner awareness of the incorporeal nature of man's being. The only image there is of God is man: God appears *as* man; but since God is incorporeal, man is incorporeal. The fact that man has a corporeal body does not make him corporeal. The fact that he travels in an airplane does not make him an airplane; and the fact that he uses and has a body does not make him a body.

Man himself is the same incorporeality that God is because they are one, not two. It is God Itself that is living man's life. That is why it is given to us, "Son, thou art ever with me, and all that I have is thine."[8] There is that word *I* again. Everything that is embodied in the word *I* is the truth about you and about me.

To live mystically, you not only must live as *I* but you cannot teach or heal except as you recognize that you are *I,* whether that *I* is sitting on one side of the table or the other.

In teaching, therefore, I am never speaking to a group of persons. I am speaking to myself and reminding myself of the truth I know. I am not addressing you: I am addressing myself, and because my Self is you, I am hearing my Self. If you think of yourself as a teacher and of someone else as a student, you will not be understood because you will be setting up twoness: the student and you. Then you will be like the righteous man who tried to get into heaven and found there was not room there. Finally he had to come to the realization that he was not himself: he was really God. Then there was room.

We use the words "teacher" and "student" merely as a kind of classification, but the moment a teacher thinks of a student as a student, he has set up the barrier of twoness and he cannot impart the message. The teacher can impart the message only when he recognizes that God is *I* and that there is only one *I:* all that *I* am imparting *I* am receiving. *I* may be imparting it as Joel and receiving it as Bill, but it is all taking place within the *I* that *I AM.*

Because of Incorporeality,
Givingness Results in Multiplication

You can easily be fooled by what is called everyday living because sooner or later somebody will tell you that you have to have common sense, and you do, when you are living out from a material state of consciousness. If, however, in an illumined state of consciousness you yield to that suggestion, you are going to lose your demonstration. It is possible to make yourself appear to have common sense to the outside world, and this you really must do because you must not try to make the unillumined understand illumination. But within yourself, do not yield to the temptation of using common sense.

For example, when you are using money—whether spending it, giving it, or doing anything else with it—do not accept the belief that you are passing it on to somebody else, because you are not. There is only one Self, and you are only transferring that money from your right-hand pocket to your left-hand pocket. You have just as much after you have given it away as you had before, because you did not give it away: you transferred it from one pocket to another, or you transferred it from one bank account to another, but it always remains in your name. What name? The name *I, I.*

"The earth is the Lord's, and the fulness thereof."[9] Therefore, although I, Joel, have nothing of my own, all that the Father has is mine. So when I give it away, it is still the Father's: it has not changed ownership. As long as I live in that consciousness, I can have infinity. I can give away infinity and still have infinity because never has its ownership or its guaranteed title been transferred from its original owner, God. As long as I can live in that consciousness, I can give, I can share, and I can impart without lessening anything of my own.

You cannot accept this until you can believe in and understand incorporeality. Let me show you how you can understand this principle in what you already know to be incorporeal. Let us take the subject of truth. I am now imparting truth. It is not mine: it is God's truth flowing through me, and I am imparting it. When I finish imparting it, will I have less truth or will I have more? You know the answer. I will have more. The very act of imparting this message is multiplying it within me. And you will say, "That is right! Truth is incorporeal; therefore, you cannot have less than you started with."

Let us take another facet of incorporeality: love. A mother loves her child, and from morning to night the parent pours love upon the child, and from night to morning. When does the mother have less love? She cannot have less love. On the contrary, by the very act of loving, she has increased her capacity for love.

And what about schoolteachers? They are always imparting knowledge. When do they begin to have less knowledge? Not as long as they are teaching, because by imparting knowledge they have more. With this you will agree. Why? It is because you are recognizing the incorporeal nature of knowledge, wisdom, truth, love.

Ah, but money! You think that is different! You have accepted a corporeal sense of supply, and so every time you spend or give a dollar, you have a dollar less, but this need not be because supply is not corporeal. Supply is your consciousness. You have entertained a false sense of supply. Once you have the sense that "the earth is the Lord's, and the fulness thereof," and all that the Father has is yours, it becomes incorporeal. The moment you understand that it is incorporeal, the more you give, the more you have.

In Healing, You Are Dealing with Incorporeal Man

Now we come back to health. As long as you accept a corporeal sense of existence, you are fighting the calendar. Every day that passes you are a day older, a day weaker, a day less alive, and because of this counting of days, months, and years, it is little wonder that the age of incapacity and all that goes with it is reached. Watch the difference when you begin to accept not only the incorporeality of God, but the incorporeality of man. Every day that you live you become younger and stronger; the more of life you use, the more you have.

Do you not see that you cannot possibly engage in a spiritual ministry while you are living out from a corporeal sense of existence? You are making a mockery of it. You are not hurting this world: You are hurting yourself.

You are setting up a barrier to the harmony of your own existence unless you can come to the place where you can say, "The only image of God I can ever see is man, and that man has to be as incorporeal as God."

When you are in this ministry, healing is not too difficult because you do not have bones to set, fevers to reduce, digestive systems to change, false appetites to get rid of, or sins to overcome, and you do not have to go around preaching to people not to smoke or drink. None of this is a part of your ministry. You are dealing with an incorporeal God manifest as an incorporeal man, and you are living, moving, and having your being in the consciousness of this.

Do not permit your ministry to descend to dealing with "man, whose breath is in his nostrils."[10] Do not tell your student or patient he should be more loving, more generous, or more kind. Do not tell him he should treat his mother-in-law better, or his wife. Do not interfere in his human affairs to any extent. Let your student or your patient present any pictures he wants to present to you, but be careful that you have the spiritual capacity not to want to change them, the spiritual faculty of discernment, the Soul-faculty. If you are a human being who has nothing more than a physical body and a mind, then of course what I am saying to you cannot make sense because you have no capacity with which to receive it.

Only Spiritual Discernment Can Reveal Incorporeality

In this ministry or in the spiritual life, unless you have this additional faculty of discernment, none of this can make sense because it is contrary to human sense, to human knowledge. When this spiritual faculty was awakened in me, a very unhappy period in my life began because I was really two persons: the "old man" was not completely "dead" and the "new man" not fully in control, and so there was a warfare between the two. Furthermore, I had not been weaned away from those who could see me only humanly and physically. Therefore, they were seeing me that way, and I was seeing them in another way. The same was true of business. I had a hard time with business. I ended up as broke as anyone has ever been, for the simple reason that I was trying to live in a corporeal sense of supply and at the same time demonstrate incorporeal supply, and it cannot be done. To attempt it is to tear yourself to pieces! It was only when I had absolutely no corporeal supply that at last I could say, "Well, now I am all right. Now I have nothing to come in conflict with." Then the flow could begin the other way.

Do not try to impart this truth too soon to anyone: to your family, your friends, neighbors, or students. Be gentle; be patient. Let them come up through the principles to where they also begin to give some evidence that they are seeing, hearing, tasting, touching, and smelling incorporeally, in other words, that they have spiritual discernment. Then, as they show forth this spiritual discernment, you can go the full route that we are taking now with those who are ready for it.

We are carrying forward the unfoldment of the incorporeality of God into the incorporeality of man, the incorporeality of body, and the incorporeality of supply. Yes, out there on our lawn is a banana tree, and at this particular moment, it has no bananas on it. Where are the bananas? One of these days they are going to be there—visible, tangible, and touchable. But where are they now? Do not tell me that they do not have existence, because they must have, or how are we ever going to see them? Before there was a seed, there was incorporeality. Even a seed has to come out of something, does it not? Out of what? From what does a seed come forth? You do not know any more than I do, except that I can tell you the name out of which it comes: the name is consciousness.

From this, you can know that all supply is incorporeal. When it appears visibly, we attach a corporeal sense to it, but it is as present now as it ever will be. Consciousness is the fabric and the substance of all form, and consciousness is incorporeal. As it manifests, we attach a corporeal sense to it, but it does not necessarily have to be that way.

Understanding Incorporeal Man Reveals the Essential Equality of Man

Many persons, in moments of spiritual discernment, have witnessed the incorporeal form of man. I, too, have beheld that incorporeal form hundreds of times, because when a person is in the Spirit, that is all he can behold. Must that not be how the idea that men are equal originally developed? Judging from appearances, no one could say that, because at all times there have been kings and slaves, generals and privates, the bond and the free, the Jew and the Greek. Always there are the literate and the illiterate; always there are the spiritual and the unspiritual. So to judge from appearances and to state that all men are equal would be rather nonsensical.

Then from whence came this vision of equality? At the beginning of the Christian era, the Greeks were the mighty intellectuals, and the Jews were the illiterate. Think of the Greeks of two thousand years ago; think of the Jews of two thousand years ago; think of the galley slaves of two thousand years ago pulling those oars; and think of Caesar. Then think what kind of a vision Paul must have had to see through the inequalities of his day; think of the spiritual vision that could say, "There is neither Jew nor Greek, there is neither bond nor free, there is neither male nor female: for ye are all one in Christ Jesus."[11]

Without spiritual intuition, you cannot see the real things of life. Without spiritual discernment, you judge only by appearances. Unless you have the spiritual vision that can perceive beyond the physical senses and see the incorporeal man and woman, see trees, fruits, and crops all as incorporeal, even though you entertain a material sense of them, the crippled man is going to stay a crippled man, and the woman taken in adultery is still going to be the woman taken in adultery.

The metaphysician who has not succeeded in the spiritual ministry, either in healing persons, demonstrating supply, or bringing forth other kinds of fruitage, has failed because he has had an incorporeal God called Spirit, and he was trying to make It manifest corporeally. And there is no corporeal creation! It is we who entertain a *corporeal sense* of an incorporeal creation!

Mysticism Is a Rising into Incorporeality

Everybody who has ever made an image of God or an image of the Christ has been guilty of idolatry, but so it is also true that everybody who has ever invented a word for God has been guilty of the same idolatry because a word is an image—only it is an image in thought. Just as a figure is an image externally, so is a word an image in thought, and anybody who is worshiping an image in thought has made for himself an idol.

To know God aright you must be unknowing, but to know man aright you must be equally unknowing. To know supply aright you must be unknowing. You must never deal with corporeality in your spiritual ministry. When you are living out from incorporeality, you have attained the mystical consciousness out of which all form appears. You may then entertain a corporeal sense of that form, but at least you will have the satisfaction of knowing that it is not corporeal. You will know that you cannot get something out of nothingness.

The fabric of life, which is consciousness and which is incorporeal, appears as incorporeal form. When you know this, even if you continue to see it corporeally, it will not fool you. Even though you handle dollar bills, you will know that you are not dealing with corporeality which is limited: you are dealing with a manifestation of supply which is infinite, and you will know that since I am *I,* it does not make any difference to whom I give it, *I* still own it, *I* still have it. I cannot give it away because it cannot get outside of the *I* that I am.

Rising to mystical consciousness in prayer and treatment means rising into incorporeality. You must begin with an incorporeal God that you cannot see, hear, taste, touch, smell, or think. Be sure of that last point: you cannot think it. You can know God aright as long as you are not thinking about God. If you stop with incorporeal God, your ministry will bring forth only the fringes of demonstration or healing. The moment you have incorporeal man and you drop his structural appearance, you will stop trying to reduce his fevers or his lumps. You will stop trying to arrest his aging processes, because incorporeal man has none. He was never born and he will never die; he was never born, so he cannot age.

When you have that man as your ministry, you must have healings. And so also you must have supply when you have incorporeal supply, consciousness as the substance of form. Whose consciousness? Mine! Yours! There is only one, only one consciousness. My consciousness, your consciousness is the substance of this universe because God is our consciousness.

This is the ultimate truth. There is nothing left to teach. You cannot go beyond incorporeality. You cannot. You have to bring forth incorporeality out of your consciousness, bring forth incorporeal man out of your own consciousness, incorporeal body and incorporeal supply.

~ 11 ~

"HIS RAIN FALLS"

Most thinking persons would be willing to admit that the majority of religious teachings of the world have not gone beyond seeking truth through the mind; but until you arrive at that place in consciousness where you realize that you never are going to find truth through the mind, you have not even begun your spiritual journey. Your journey begins only when you come to the realization that going on as you have been, you never are going to learn the truth—what lies behind this universe—because it is not to be known with the mind.

Think back a few years in your experience and try to remember what it was that first brought you to the spiritual path. Was it primarily for a healing or for some other aspect of better humanhood? Or was it an actual desire, a search, a reaching out for Reality, for Truth, for God? Since that time, to what extent has your attitude changed? Do you realize that merely improving health or increasing the amount of your supply is insignificant in comparison with the goal of finding the mystery of that Life that is behind the appearance, behind what you see, hear, taste, touch, and smell?

True, there are times when it is discouraging, because inevitably the realization comes: "Am I never going to discover God or Spirit? Is my search to be completely frustrating? What have I to look forward to?" Reaching that point may be a good start on your spiritual journey because you will have arrived at that place where you can say, "Speak, Lord; for thy servant heareth,"[1] and mean it, really mean that if God does not speak and if you do not hear what He says, there is going to be no answer. When you reach that place, it means that you have come to the end of faith and hope and any belief that the human mind is ever going to reveal spiritual truth to you.

At that point in consciousness, you do know that God is not going to be revealed to you in the words that you read or the words that you hear. The only opportunity for God to be revealed to you, even through your relationship with your spiritual teacher, is in what his consciousness can impart and what your consciousness can receive, independent of words and thoughts. There must be a relationship between teacher and student that transcends words and thoughts; there must be a state of consciousness that can receive that which an attained spiritual consciousness can impart. The teacher can impart truth without words or thoughts, but as a rule, he will do this by means of words and thoughts and let the Spirit do the actual imparting, that is, carry the import of the message.

God Neither Punishes Nor Rewards

When *The Thunder of Silence*[2] was published, I knew that I could not expect many people in the world to understand or grasp it, not even our students. I did not expect it then, and I do not expect this understanding to come for many, many years. That is because it is a complete contradiction of every teaching that is based on God's goodness to you and God's punishment of the sinner.

Probably some of you have lived long enough, however, to find out that God has not been too good to you, and probably some of you have discovered that God does not really punish sinners at all: they seem to go scot-free. Once in a while the law catches up with one of them, and he is sent to jail, but God does not seem to have anything to do with that: it is due to the alertness of the police department.

You must be puzzled and startled, too, when you know how many sweet, loving, good, charitable persons there are in the world whom God is not rewarding, and it must amaze you to see the number of evil persons there are whom the law not only has not yet reached, but on whom even God has not put his finger. You must wonder about this, and then wonder if the churches' explanation is a valid one, that if you do not get punished here, you will get punished somewhere else—not that anyone has come back to prove his point that there is a hell or any other place where sinners are punished afterward.

So it is that the longer you seek the answer with your mind, the more frustrating this is going to be, and if you do not have an answer to it, you may be assured that not only will your frustration in life continue, but the solution to life's problems will not be given you. When the first unfoldment of the truth that God does not reward nor does He punish came through my lips, it startled me as much as it did any of those who were listening and who caught it. It was not anything that I had known even five minutes before, and be assured I had to do a great deal of thinking and meditating after that message came through to realize the astounding nature of what it was. Search the literature of the world and see what a startling revelation it is to announce that God neither punishes nor rewards. Why, it refutes most of the religious teachings of the world.

As Ye Sow

Since God neither punishes nor rewards and since there is, as we all know, a certain amount of punishment and reward that goes on in this world, what is the answer? The answer that came through was what the Hindus call karmic law, or what has been called the law of as-ye-sow-so-shall-ye-reap. This throws the Christian teaching that God punishes and rewards out the window because if it is true that you reap what you sow, then punishment and reward have nothing to do with God. They have to do with a law that you set in motion. Paul gave the revelation which he received from the Christ: "For he that soweth to his flesh shall of the flesh reap corruption; but he that soweth to the Spirit shall of the Spirit reap life everlasting."[3] Here is given the basic Christian teaching.

If you can catch this principle which is a major revelation found in *The Thunder of Silence* and come to a conviction within yourself that insofar as your rewards and punishments are concerned you can leave God out of your calculations, then you can make this acknowledgment, "Regardless of where I am in life, regardless of what experience I may now be having, somewhere or other there was a sowing in my consciousness that is responsible for this reaping." To grasp this teaching of the Infinite Way is to be halfway home.

If you are still probing around in your mind, hoping for God to do something or change something, you are not adhering to the principles of Jesus, and you are still waiting for that which is not going to happen. Whatever is going to happen is going to happen as an activity of your consciousness.

This is a subject with which you will have to work for at least a year or two, if you have not already done so, until you come to the full realization of the startling nature of what I am saying to you. At this moment, it may not seem startling to you at all, but that is only because you have not grasped the full significance of it. When you can wholly understand the meaning of this, the rest is going to be easy, because operating in the consciousness of most persons and causing unnecessary distress, there is a belief that some act of commission or omission on their part is responsible for their discords or inharmonies.

It is not that way at all, and you may as well forgive yourself right now and forget about your past or present sins of commission or omission. Forgive yourself by recognizing the impersonal nature of evil, and drop out of your thought right now that it was any error of yours, *except an ignorance of spiritual principles,* that brought about your problems. I am not speaking primarily to you who already have come a great part of the way along this Path, but I am reminding you of what you must be revealing to your students in order to free them from their guilt complexes and from the belief that they should be expecting a reward for the good things they have done in life or a punishment for the bad things that they may have done or the good things they have left undone. You must set them free. In a great measure you, yourself, have perhaps already been set free by your studies and work, but remember, I am merely giving this to you so that you may complete your demonstration and so that you may have the full awareness of this principle in dealing with those who come to you.

Relying on Effect Is Sowing to the Flesh

Then what is the sowing and the reaping that is causing the distress of so many people on this earth? Paul summed it up, and we will have to do what he probably did, but which never got into print: we will have to explain what he merely stated. "For he that soweth to his flesh shall of the flesh reap corruption; but he that soweth to the Spirit shall of the Spirit reap life everlasting."

That is the statement, and the explanation is this: You were born into a material sense of life, therefore, you have been sowing to the flesh all your human life. In other words, you have put your entire hope, faith, and confidence in form or effect. You have been brought up to believe that money is supply, and it is this teaching that really causes all the lack and limitation on earth because whether you believe that money is supply, or crops, it is equally an error. Just to be born into the belief that money, investments, securities, jobs, professions, and business are supply makes you go out to try to get these, and thereby cheats you of the demonstration of supply because these are not supply.

Consciousness is supply; Spirit is supply; the Invisible is supply. Supply is That over which you have no control, but That which can, when you permit it, control, govern, and fulfill you. When you go far enough in the message of the Infinite Way, you will discover that *I* am supply, that *I* within you embody and embrace the infinity of supply, not only for your own use, but that *I* can feed five thousand, because *I* is God. "I am the bread of life"[4]–the meat, the wine, the water. "I am the resurrection, and the life.[5] . . . Whosoever drinketh of the water that I shall give him shall never thirst."[6]

Until you actually accept that, you are going to be sowing to the flesh and you are going to reap limitation. True, there are persons who reap a million dollars' worth of limitation, and ten million dollars' worth of limitation. Nevertheless, it is limitation, and the proof of that is that after they get their millions, sometimes they cannot eat twenty-five cents worth of food, and sometimes they cannot spend any of it. They have to sit and watch it, count it, and gloat over it as it multiplies, and they can no more part with it than they could part with their own blood. Money, in and of itself, cannot spend itself. It takes the spirit of a man to part with it, to share it, to give it, to distribute it. The money itself will not do that.

To Be Born into an Unillumined Family Is to Be Born into Limitation

To be born into the average family, therefore, means to be born into the strife and struggle of earning a living; whereas to be born into a family of spiritual understanding means that from the very beginning a child would be taught to sow to the Spirit, to realize that love and life are supply, that God is supply, that *I* am supply. That child would grow up with such a different concept of supply that he would never struggle, lie, or cheat for it, but whatever activity he undertook, whether that of an artist, doctor, lawyer, designer, or builder, he would be doing it for the joy of life; he would be doing it as a gift of God, as the grace of God.

It makes little difference what work a person is doing in life, it becomes a joy the moment he is not doing it merely for a living. When he is doing it for a living, he cannot help but watch the clock, wondering whether he is giving more than he is getting. When, however, he does not connect supply with his livelihood, then his activity, whatever it may be, becomes such a joy that he is giving himself to it. He is sowing to the Spirit, and supply then may come through that avenue, but it may also come through many, many others.

In the same way, if you were born into a typical family, what were the first words you heard? What else but "Be careful! Do not drop the baby! Do not leave the baby in a draft!" And you did not hear those words only with your ears: they went deep into your consciousness. From that second on, you can be assured you were sowing to the flesh: you were watching the body; you were careful not to sit in a draft or to get your feet wet; you were fearful of germs. In other words, you were doing something that made you apprehensive of the body.

One of the first things a youngster learns when he goes to school is, "Do not talk to a stranger, he might be a kidnaper." So a fear of kidnapers goes into the mind of every child, whereas very few children ever meet one, probably only one in ten million. Do you see how a child is learning to sow to the flesh, instead of being taught from the beginning, "These people are your brothers and sisters. These are children of God"? Oh, no, no! This stranger might be a kidnaper, and even if not, he probably does not belong to your church, and that makes it bad; and he may not belong to your race or your nation, and that makes it worse.

Do you not see what I mean by sowing to the flesh? It has nothing to do with your personal sins. Your personal sins and mine are due to the fact that we were born into this consciousness that sows to the flesh. Therefore, one thing became a pleasure of the flesh, and another became a pain of the flesh; this became desirable to the flesh, and that became undesirable to the flesh. And what is happening? What has happened? All you have done is to cater to the flesh.

Now what of the Spirit? How many of you have heard of that? Who ever heard of the invisible Spirit that is in us, this invisible Spirit which is the Spirit of God in man? Who ever directed your attention to the Spirit of God in your neighbor, or to the Spirit of God in the sinner? Who ever directed your attention to the fact that not only the saints but all the sinners have the same Spirit of God in them, and that it is only your ignorance of this truth that brings upon you the discords of the flesh, even the diseases?

Recognizing the Invisible

Are you living on the materialistic plane of consciousness that has all its hopes, ambitions, fears, loves, and hates in the external world? Or do you perceive that behind this visible universe there is an invisible spiritual presence, power, and law? Do you understand that that which is made and is visible is really made of that which is Invisible?

The multiplication of coconuts on a coconut tree is dependent, not on the tree, but on an invisible Source that operates in the tree, through it, upon it, and ultimately as the tree. The world calls it a force of nature without ever knowing what a force of nature is. Actually it is a name given to the unknown invisible Activity that produces fruit where there was none before.

If your sowing is entirely on the materialistic plane, your reaping must be on that plane, and since everything in the material realm is constituted of both good and evil, it means that there will be times when you will have good and abundant material activity and other times when you will have bad and insufficient material activity. You will be volleying back and forth between good and evil, abundance and lack, sickness and health, life and death.

To sow to the Spirit means that even while you go through your human sense of life in the same way as you have heretofore, outwardly performing the same tasks, being about the Father's business in whatever way it has been given you to do, you will be recognizing that God is really the law of your activity:

Within me, though invisible, is the presence and power of God. Within me is the kingdom of God, the allness of God. I do not know how It operates: I only know that there is a Spirit in man, and that Spirit within me is the son of God, my true Selfhood.

This Spirit of God is within me for a specific purpose: to heal the sick, to raise the dead, to feed the hungry, to forgive the sinner. It is here to go before me to "make the crooked places straight."[7] *It is here to go before me to reveal "mansions"*[8] *to me. It walks beside me, and behind me.*

This son of God within me, this spiritual Presence, is here to govern my day. It is my food, clothing, and housing; It is the source of my inspiration; It is that which governs, guides, protects, and leads me through the activity of my entire day.

When you partake of any food that is set before you, do so in the conscious realization of the *source*, so that you do not fall into the trap of believing that it is your money that buys that food for you, or your position. Actually, if you had all the millions of a Rockefeller, you could not produce a single potato without the activity of God. Not all the money in the world will make one single carrot or an egg—not one. Only the grace of God can do that. You must constantly know that there is an Invisible, and that it is this Invisible within you that produces your daily bread. This takes egotism away, and with it the pride of possession.

People who drive automobiles often pride themselves on being good drivers, and they even boast that they have not had an accident for so and so many years. But that is a poor thing on which to place reliance. To realize, however, that within every driver on the road is the grace and presence of God is to place your reliance where it belongs, and then if a driver does make a mistake or err in judgment, there is this divine Presence to correct him, awaken him, change his course, or do what is necessary to be done.

Sowing to the flesh means putting your faith in the visible world: in machinery, in dollar bills, securities, or governments, in "man, whose breath is in his nostrils"[9]; whereas sowing to the Spirit has always meant acknowledging the spiritual as being the basis of the harmony of the visible. It is to acknowledge spiritual power in all your ways, acknowledge spiritual law as governing you from morning to night and night to morning, acknowledge Spirit as the substance, the law, the activity, and the reality of being. Then you will be praying without ceasing, and you will be knowing the truth that makes you free.

Spiritual Ignorance Is the Barrier

If it were not so ingrained in most human beings to fear weather, climate, germs, and infection, they would not have half the things wrong with them that most persons have. So it is not their personal sins: it is that which they have accepted of the universal belief through their ignorance. Ignorance is the major sin.

Only the ignorant remain out of heaven or harmony. The sinner gets into heaven the moment he is enlightened because then there is no more sin, and a person who is not sinning is not a sinner. What happened yesterday, last week, last month, or last year is gone because "though your sins be as scarlet, they shall be as white as snow."[10] The basic Christian teaching is that you are white as snow in that very moment when your ignorance is overcome and you begin to realize: "Any wrong that I have done of a major or minor nature was based on my ignorance. That is all! Had there been enlightenment, it could never have happened." How do you know that? Enlightened persons do not do wrong. It is an impossibility for a spiritually enlightened person to do wrong. Why? Because there is nothing in all this world worth having enough to commit a wrong to get.

What is it that you could possibly want out in the world when you have the kingdom of God within? You do not have to lie, cheat, steal, or defraud to obtain supply because when you realize the nature of supply, it begins to flow. Pleasures? Who has to cheat for pleasures, when all the pleasure there is in the world is unfolding from within, and if it takes another person or if it takes six others to provide that pleasure, they will be provided. There is no need to go out looking for them.

Karmic Law on a National Level

You would be surprised what happens in your personal life when you come to an actual realization that there is nothing good or evil in "this world."[11] It is only habit, custom, belief, or tradition that makes it so. Things that are right in one place are wrong in another place; things that are moral in one place are immoral in another place.

With only a small percentage of the workers in the United States engaged in agriculture today, more food is being produced, not only more than this nation can consume, but more than all the nations that are buying from us can afford to pay for, and still the storehouses are full. A major reason for our overabundance must be know-how, understanding, knowledge, and one reason for the lack in some other countries must be lack of know-how.

Then do you not see that it is not really God that has provided us with our great abundance of crops as a reward for our virtues, nor is God punishing other nations by limiting the amount of their crops? It is just a matter of sowing and reaping. If those nations that have an overabundance were to share freely with those that have not, eventually it would bring about an abundance for all nations, and the situation in the world would be very different. But can that be while any person or nation is sowing to the flesh and believing, "Oh, no, no! I am rich while I have it in the storehouse, even though it may be rotting there"?

Sowing to the flesh reaps corruption because sometimes sowing to the flesh reaps an overabundance, and that overabundance corrupts the morals and certainly corrodes the soul. Can it help corroding the soul of a person or nation to know that he or it has an overabundance and somebody else is starving? Can it help hurting? Of course not!

In our individual experience, if we are sowing to the Spirit, such an experience cannot come to us. We cannot be corrupted because freely we can give. We cannot give away what belongs to another, to the government or to our neighbor, so we cannot keep it or him from its or his own reaping, but individually we need not sow to the flesh to the extent of believing that we must withhold while others are in lack. We can be as free as our own Spirit permits, proving thereby that we are sowing to the Spirit and not to the flesh.

Not only is every individual sowing, but every nation is sowing and will reap the karma of its own actions until there is a new kind of sowing. If you do not understand this law of karma, you will not understand the reason, not only for the sufferings of many Americans individually, but for the failure to arrive at a satisfactory solution to some of the major problems confronting the world today. Unless you understand this law, you, as a citizen, cannot help to bring forth harmony.

We individually and the government as a government must acknowledge guilt in the areas of anti-Semitism, in the racial problem in the South and in some parts of the North, in the persecution of the Japanese in California during World War II, and last but not least, in the use by the United States of the atomic bomb. Until you, as an individual, come to an inner agreement that destroying civilian populations by atomic bombs is inexcusable, you are under that karma, because the commands to "resist not evil"[12] and to lay down your life rather than take another life are basic Christian teachings. Certainly the teaching was never to save your life at the expense of another's.

As long as governments have adopted warfare as a part of normal Christian living, you will have to accept your responsibility as a citizen, but to accept within your consciousness the rightness of it brings you under the law of sowing to the flesh. If you believe that it is right to protect your property or your life at the expense of someone else's life or to destroy a civilian population to win a war, you are sowing to the flesh, and there is no way to experience anything other than that karma. By this, I do not mean that you are necessarily to voice this publicly, but that you as an individual inwardly must come out from under this karma and agree within yourself that you cannot lend your approval to these things.

Inwardly, you must come to that place in consciousness where you cannot believe in the rightness of taking another person's life. Then you, individually, have come out from under that karma, but until your nation through its government likewise voices its disapproval of racial persecution, religious persecution, or the wanton destruction of civilian life in warfare, it still is under the law of karma, not under any law of punishment or reward from God. No, God has never been responsible for any evil that has ever touched this world. The fault does not lie in God. God has not visited evil upon His children.

The story of Noah and the Ark is not the story of a God who saved out one individual and destroyed all the rest in the world. It is an account of the operation of karmic law. So, in any age, where a people or a nation is living contrary to the principle of loving "thy neighbor as thyself,"[13] it can eventually expect a flood, a flood of water or a flood of bombs, but a flood of one nature or another that will wipe the evil away, even if it has to take their human sense of life along with it. But it is not God. Do not place the responsibility upon God! Release God:

Never again will I fear God; never again will I place the responsibility for my ills upon God. God is too pure to behold iniquity, and this I will maintain with every breath of my being. God has no awareness of whatever it is that is disturbing me. God has no awareness of the evil in my mind, the disease in my body, or the lack in my pocketbook.

Reject the temptation to think of God in connection with any of the evils of your world or anyone else's world. Reject it instantly, and then you will be set free for the next step, which is the realization:

The only substance this evil has is the carnal mind, the belief in two powers. But now there no longer is any belief in two powers entertained in my consciousness. There cannot be two powers in a purely spiritual universe created by a pure God: there cannot be both good and evil in God.

"Hear, O Israel: The Lord our God is one Lord."[14] God is one and God is love: not a combination of good and evil, not a combination of reward and punishment. God is one.

As you work with this understanding of God and of karma, of sowing and reaping, remember that to receive enlightenment you have to open your consciousness to receive the impartations of the Spirit. Then will begin your spiritual life. This first part brings you up to good humanhood, perfect humanhood, but then you must open yourself to receive spiritual impartations through the new consciousness that you have developed. In that consciousness, karma is surmounted because there is no longer any sowing, and therefore, no longer any reaping. You are no longer the doer: you are the instrument as which God is performing His mighty works.

~ 12 ~

GOD REVEALING HIMSELF
AS CHRIST ON EARTH

Regardless of the heights we may attain on the spiritual path, it does not mean that we will forever be without problems of one kind or another. It is safe to say from what we have observed that most of the problems of those who are on the Path will be minor ones and easily resolved. Occasionally, however, because of universal world hypnotism, some very, very severe problems come even to the student of a considerable measure of spiritual attainment.

The mere fact that we are living in a world with other people means that we cannot close our eyes to the troubles and problems of our friends or families. Sometimes, too, we cannot close our eyes to the troubles and problems of the world, and so, as we come under the hypnotism of world belief, we may encounter a serious problem at any stage of our spiritual experience.

No matter how great the problem may be, however, even that of facing death, it does not seem too great because we have come to the realization that life here or life there is still life, so that it is just going to be a matter of making the adjustment to life on one plane of life or another. Of course, when the world faces serious problems, it has no answer, and that is a terrifying spot to be in: to face serious problems and to realize there are no answers.

We have one great advantage, however, over the rest of the world and over those persons who live in fear of every pain because they think it is a sign that they are going to die. We do know that there is an answer, and that it is just a matter of our attaining that answer. And what is the answer? The right degree of spiritual realization. So we have something toward which to work because we know that if we were facing our last minute of life on earth, it could be completely reversed, just by the correct realization.

I do want to make this point, however, that probably those on this Path are free of eighty per cent of all the world's problems, and the twenty per cent that might touch them, they meet quickly. And those few that they do not meet, they will meet as consciousness unfolds. In fact, all problems will be met eventually on this plane or the next, so that no problem should be of too serious concern to us.

Right Identification

What differentiates the life of the person who experiences good and evil—health and sickness, abundance and lack, purity and sin, happiness and unhappiness—from the life of the person of spiritual attainment, whose life is on the whole a continuity of harmony, is the matter of right identification.

Right identification is a recognition of the truth that *I* is God and the ability not to think out from the standpoint of being man, limited and subject to human laws. While we know that about 500 B.C. Gautama the Buddha had this revelation, we do not know too much of the nature of that revelation or how he presented it, but we do know that even before the time of Gautama, Moses gave the full and complete revelation to the world in his words: "*I AM THAT I AM.*"[1] This transformed him from a shepherd into the leader and the liberator of the Hebrew people, and endowed him with sufficient spiritual power to take them out from under the nose of Pharaoh and lead them to the Promised Land.

He could not take them *into* the Promised Land. Nobody can take anyone into the Promised Land: he can only reveal this truth to him, but if he is unable to accept it, he cannot enter that Land. Nobody can take another person into the Promised Land as long as he thinks there is God *and* man—nobody! A spiritual teacher can lead a person to greater heights by instructing him, but it is the person himself who must attain the realization, "Oh, *I AM*," and then he walks right into the Promised Land. In fact, he finds himself in the very middle of it.

"I and my Father," who always have been one, then become one in realization. "I and my Father are one"[2] is the realized relationship between God and man. There are not two: there is one. The life of God is the life of man. God breathed His life into man—not man's life: God breathed God's life into man. Therefore, the life of man is God.

God Revealing Himself on Earth

One of the evils of the human world is that it looks on human conception as if it were something human, sometimes even evil or sinful, and at best, physical. This misses the whole point because it is not sinful: it is something sacred. It is another individualization of God appearing. In that light, it is not a human being that is born, and it is not the product of a carnal act that has taken place. It is I and the Father becoming one, and out of that oneness is coming another one.

When our young married couples, through spiritual study, realize this, and realize that the process of conception is not a carnal act, not something to be afraid of or ashamed of or merely an act of pleasure, but that actually it is a natural function of life, then they will discover that the seed will be held as something sacred. It will be buried in the womb, and it will be held there sacredly and secretly as if they were waiting now for God to appear, for the Christ to incarnate. All those months of gestation of Mary is the waiting for the Christ, the son of God, to appear. When young married people approach the bringing forth of a child with the understanding that they are waiting for the incarnation of the Christ to appear, parentage will be looked upon as a trust, children will be held as something sacred, and we will begin living spiritually on earth.

Many persons would like to believe that if they are spiritual there will be no sex relationships, but if that is so, then they will be so spiritual that they will not have to eat or drink, and I do not believe that for a while any one of us is going to reach that point. I do believe that our spiritual life for a long time to come is going to be lived on earth, and the method of this progressive unfoldment of life will be as it is now, only instead of being thought of as just a human act, it is now going to be understood as God's way of revealing Himself, or His son, on earth. It is God's way of expressing Christhood on earth. The whole of this life is going to be sacred the moment it is known that *I* is God.

The Infinite Nature of Consciousness

God did not give man a mind: the mind of God becomes the mind of man, and it is for this reason that we can receive impartations of a spiritual nature from within if we are interested in the spiritual things of life, or that we can bring forth ideas for telephones, radios, television, automobiles, airplanes, and all the things that have not yet been discovered if that is the direction in which our talent lies. Why? Because they are embodied in our consciousness. They have always been embodied in the consciousness of man. They were embodied in the consciousness of Christopher Columbus, Leonardo da Vinci, Michelangelo, Thomas Edison, Henry Ford, and many others.

An artist, if he is a real artist, does not go to art galleries to look at pictures and then go home and copy what he has seen. A musician who is a real composer does not go around listening to other composers' music and then go home and try to imitate what he has heard. The artist, the composer, and the writer go within their consciousness and out of it bring forth their art, music, and literature. Why? Their consciousness is infinite because God constitutes their consciousness, and by closing their eyes and going within, they are going to God and thereby have access to ideas unto infinity.

The Master revealed this principle when he said, "The kingdom of God cometh not with observation: Neither shall they say, Lo here! or lo there!"[3] It is not up in some holy mountain; it is not even in the holy temple in Jerusalem. "The kingdom of God is within you!"[3] And what does the world do? It continues to look for holy mountains, holy temples, and holy teachers, instead of accepting what Moses revealed, what Elijah, Isaiah, Jesus, Paul, John, and Buddha revealed, and how many others I cannot even tell you because it has been known to so many.

The truth is that what *I AM* is, *we are,* and all that *I AM* is, *we are.* "All that I have is thine."[4] This, God reveals so that we do not make the mistake of pleading with God for something. "All that I have is thine." How can we look to God for anything? That we can never do if we are abiding in the Word, *I AM.*

Over and over, the Infinite Way writings repeat the Master's words: " I have meat to eat that ye know not of "[5]:

I *have hidden manna.* I *will never leave me, nor forsake me.* I *was with me before the world began.* I *will be with me unto the end of the world.*

Whatever it is that I have even thought that I needed or wanted, I have only had to go within my own being, and if I have been still and patient, the assurance has come:

"It is I; *be not afraid."* [6] I *am thy bread, thy meat, thy wine, thy water.* "I *will never leave thee, nor forsake thee."* [7]

It always comes from within; it always has. Ever since my first spiritual experience, that has been my way of life. Every time that I have seemed to be separated from any sense of good or any form of good, I have only had to go within for the realization of that *I* within me, and then the assurance is given me: "*I* go before thee to make the crooked places straight."

The Indissoluble Union

The basic principle of the Infinite Way is in the word *I*. The teaching, as set forth in the textbook *The Infinite Way*,[8] is that God appears as man–not God *and* man, not man going to God, but the revelation that God appears *as* man. Then all that God is, I am; all that the Father has is mine, and so the way to find that God lies in going within to that *I* that I am.

The importance of realizing the nature of God, and more especially realizing the nature of God *as* our own being, so that the universal belief that there is God *and* man is broken down by the realization that God is manifest *as* man, has always been emphasized in the Infinite Way. Now it is presumed that students are ready for the *realization* rather than merely the teaching of this principle. It is one thing to be taught or even to teach something: it is quite a different thing to *be* that, to attain the consciousness of that which has been taught.

It has been taught for two thousand years that "I and my Father are one," yet very few persons have attained any measure of awareness of that relationship with Deity. "I and my Father are one" means that I am that One. "He that seeth me seeth him that sent me,"[9] but how far short we fall from realizing that we are that He and from living out from the basis of being Spirit, rather than a man seeking Spirit.

Seventeen years of presenting the message of the Infinite Way in many, many different forms has gradually lifted consciousness above the belief of separation from God to the attainment of a consciousness through which we are enabled to say, "Whereas I was blind, now I see"[10]–I am He. This enables us to take the higher stand and the higher step of abiding constantly and consciously in the realization of *I*. With every temptation to accept ourselves as a selfhood apart from God, with every temptation to accept others as having a selfhood apart from God, we must immediately retire into that word *I* and abide in it: *I* am He, *I* am every "he," "she," and "it," because I am that *I AM*. That spiritual identity, *I*, I am.

Knowing this, ask yourself: Can I be tempted to accept the universal belief that my good can come to me from anywhere, from anyone, from any power, from any being? Or do I realize that by voicing the word *I*, I am declaring the divinity of my being, and therefore, the all-inclusiveness of my being, so that I cannot *receive* bread, meat, wine, or water, I cannot *be* resurrected, I cannot *become* life eternal. Why? Because *I* am the bread, the meat, the wine, the water; *I* am the resurrection; *I* am life eternal; *I* am He. The very good that should come to me, *I* embody. *I* embrace the infinity of being in the consciousness which *I* am.

The Tempter

Regardless of the nature of the temptation that would present itself to you and cause you to try to demonstrate supply, health, safety, or security, you must remember why the Master revealed his own temptations to the disciples, and the way in which he handled those temptations. " 'Get thee behind me,'[11] temptation, or tempter, for I do not have to demonstrate bread. I do not have to turn stones into bread; I do not have to demonstrate safety; I do not have to depend on a God to protect me. I have realized that I and the Father are one, and all that the Father has is mine. Therefore, I have bread without the necessity of demonstrating it; I have safety and security without proving it or testing myself or seeking it from God."

As a matter of fact, Jesus was indicating that he had come to the realization that there was no God outside of himself that could give him bread or safety, even if he jumped off the cliff, for the safety as well as the bread was included in the consciousness which he was. So he was virtually denying any God or any power separate and apart from his own consciousness.

We are called upon every day of our lives to bear witness to this revelation because whether or not we may need any immediate supply, there are those who come to us in person, by cable, by telephone, or through the mail, presenting to us the claim of lack and limitation. To them, we can have only one answer: "The *I* that I am, thou art. Therefore, the fullness of the Godhead bodily which is the fulfillment of my being is the fulfillment of thy being, since there is but one *I*, one infinite Being, regardless of how many times It may be manifested on earth." Every time that the tempter comes to me or to you, or to any "you" anywhere, we must bear witness to the truth of *I*, to the truth of our oneness with the Father, to the infinity of all that the Father is, embodied in the *I* that we are.

In dealing with mental, physical, moral, as well as financial problems, the answer is the same: "This is the tempter appearing to me, claiming that we are man, whatever that word 'man' may mean." That is the whole temptation. The temptation is not that we lack or that we are sick, or have no integrity, or are immoral. The temptation is to accept ourselves as man. If I accept you as man, I accept all the limitations that go with that identity, and then I can hardly deny that you may suffer from sin, sickness, lack, limitation, unhappiness, or any other of the world's claims that afflict man. There is only one tempter, Satan, or devil, and that is the impersonal universal belief. But there is only one temptation, and that is to accept yourself and myself as other than the *I* that we are.

Moses saw through the temptation. He realized, *"I AM THAT I AM."* And then the Master many years later realized, "I am the way, the truth, and the life."[12] He revealed this to the world as universal truth, not merely the truth about himself, for he said, "If I bear witness of myself, my witness is not true."[13] Therefore, this must be the truth about every "you" in all the world, since your Father is my Father, and my Father is your Father. We have but one Father. We—you and I, and every other "you"—are the one son, established in the same sonship. The truth about me is the truth about you, for I speak and bear witness to my Father and your Father. I bear witness to sonship, my sonship and your sonship. I am heir of God, and you are heir of God, joint-heir, not to a little bit of heaven, but to *all* of the heavenly riches.

From the beginning, *I* and the Father have coexisted in a spiritual relationship that was established "before Abraham was."[14] *I* have always lived in the bosom of the Father, and even when *I* went forth to walk on earth, *I* never left the Father because *I* and the Father are inseparable and indivisible. Let none of us ever voice what the Master said, but let us all recognize and realize that this is the truth: "He that seeth me seeth him that sent me. . . . [for] I and my Father are one."

Since you know that God is Spirit, then you know that all that the Father has must be spiritual. God is

Spirit, and you must worship God in Spirit and in truth. When you go to God, therefore, go for what may be called the gifts of God, the grace of God. And what are these? Do not worry what they are; do not be concerned. Just go for God's grace.

"The kingdom of God is within you,"[15] the *I* of you is God, so turn within to this *I* for Its grace and Its peace. "My peace I give unto you: not as the world giveth."[16] Do not ever forget that the Master's "My peace" is not the peace that the world gives. Those who want only the world's peace must find their own way of getting it because they will never get anything like that from God.

But we do want the peace that God can give. Then the moment we turn within for God's grace, God's peace, even that the Spirit of God may be upon us, we are no longer dependent on, nor are we at the mercy of, "man, whose breath is in his nostrils."[17] When the Spirit of God is upon us, we are ordained, ordained to be the spiritual son.

In our humanhood, we are not children of God. Our little personal "I" is not God, or we all would be individual gods walking around, and none of us would ever be in trouble. In our humanhood, we are "the natural man" that Paul revealed "receiveth not the things of the Spirit of God."[18] That "natural man" is not under the law of God. That is why he can sin and have sinful appetites; that is why he can be diseased; that is why he can be uncharitable and unmerciful. There is nothing godlike about him: he is an animal, virtually a beast. That is what is wrong with this whole human race. It can go to church and pray from now until doomsday, and if it is not careful, the roof of the church will fall in on it.

The End of the Search

When, however, an individual in one way or another is led to the search for God, this means that *something* within him is trying to break through. When we know this, we can stop our search for God and sit down and listen more, and then God will break through. The search for God never ends until we realize, "I and my Father are one," "*I* am thou," or "I will never leave thee, nor forsake thee." Whether it comes as a message, whether it is spoken in the ear, or whether it is just an inner experience, the moment that *I* voices Itself, we know that that *I* is not man: that *I* is God.

Now we relax and rest in that *I* in that *I AM.* Now we do not have to take thought for our life, what we shall eat, what we shall drink, or wherewithal we shall be clothed. Now we rest, and life begins to be lived out from within the Self. Then it is that we are a benediction to all who come within range of our thought, not because we are walking around blessing anybody, but because, as we look at the persons who cross our path, we are realizing that *I* at the center of their being. We cannot help it. There is a smile that comes to us when we stop to think, "Oh, you may not know it, but I know that the kingdom of God is within you."

Infinite Individuality Fulfilled

You would be surprised how many receptive persons there are, how many there are with an inner longing whom that recognition awakens. You may never know them personally; you may never know whom you have blessed, although here and there you will find someone who will say, "I feel something in you." What is it he feels in you? Only one thing: your understanding of your true identity and your understanding of his true identity. That is what he feels. You are no longer looking on him with criticism, judgment, malice, hate, or unforgiveness. This you cannot do any more. You look out at this whole world with compassion: "I know what it is all about now. You thought you were man; you thought you were living your own experience. If you did not have money, you may have felt that you had to steal, cheat, or lie. If only you had known *I,* you would have relaxed and, without taking thought, your own would have come to you."

John Burroughs could give the world his inspiring poem, "Waiting," with its theme of confidence and assurance, "My own shall come to me," because he had attained the consciousness of that. As a human being, no one can ever say, "My own shall come to me." A human being has to go out and fight for whatever he gets, struggle for it, labor for it. It is only when spiritual realization comes that he can sit by the side of a stream and know that his own will come to him. It will find him employment, give him talent, or whatever it is that is required to fulfill his life—and find him wherever he may be.

It is important for every student to remember that *I* is God, but also that *I* appears as every person individually, as much so as fingerprints. In other words, no two of us are the same. No two of us are required to do the same work; no two of us are supposed to express art, literature, music, or salesmanship in the same way. Each one of us has an individual gift. Thousands of us may play the piano or the violin, but if we have made contact with our Center, each one will play it in an individual way, so individual that the same music played by a Hoffman will sound different when played by a Paderewski. A painter, sculptor, or writer will express himself in individual forms of beauty, art, or literature. But this can come about only when we, as individuals, begin to understand that *I* in the midst of us is mighty, *I* in the midst of us is infinite, because *I* in the midst of us is God.

Every person who has not fully attained that realization must turn within to the *I* at the Center, to the Consciousness, and then forth from this Consciousness will come whatever is necessary to his individual unfoldment, which may not in any way be another's unfoldment. Everyone has to go within to the Center of his being, the Consciousness of his own being, and draw forth that which represents the fulfillment of his individuality.

Secrecy Imperative

Live in the word *I*. But be careful, be careful! It has always been lost by revealing It to the unprepared thought—always, always! It has made some persons believe that they humanly had power or were powerful: "Oh, I am God," and then they began to try to be God, and they destroyed themselves. There have been movements down through the ages that have broken up, begun again and broken up every time some group that was not ready for it learned this secret. They thought that it meant personal power, or that it could make one person a power over another, or a power over his nation. That is not its meaning. No one becomes a power over anyone else: he becomes a transparency for the power of Spirit, the power of love, the power of life, the power of liberty–not a power over the personal life of anyone.

Be still! "Be still, and know that I am God."[19] It is on this point that secrecy must become the absolute law with you. I tell you that if you reveal it you will lose it, and you will be sorry because you may not regain it in this entire lifetime on earth. Therefore, do not reveal it to the unprepared thought. It may be taught and imparted to the student as Jesus and Gautama the Buddha both did with their disciples, and secrecy is not violated, because those students who are drawn to a spiritual teacher become one with the teacher: one consciousness, one mind, and one life.

It is not possible to know this truth and live a personal life for yourself. To some extent your life will have to be dedicated, but do not let it be dedicated to telling this to anyone until, in the course of time, you find students and become convinced that they are not looking for "loaves and fishes" or how to rule the world, but how to be a greater dedication to the world than they already are. Then is when you can gently, gently, very gently lead up to this point. If you will read the Infinite Way books again, you will see how gently I have led up to this great truth in every one of the books. It has been touched so lightly that only those who have eyes to see will see it, and only those who have ears will hear it.

Never share your spiritual experiences, although from now on, normally and naturally, you should have more of them than you have had, and if you have had none, you should begin to have them. But keep those experiences within yourself. Do not share them with anyone.

Your teacher, yes; your practitioner, yes, but not husband, wife, friend, or relative because no one but your teacher is at your state of unfoldment when you are having those experiences, and therefore no one is going to be able to understand them. Keep them within yourself, and let them multiply, let them deepen, let them become enriched. Never fear them, although some of them come in a form that is sometimes frightening because those things with which we are unfamiliar arouse a fear in us, but there is nothing to be afraid of if we are in God and if God is revealing Himself.

Secrecy in spiritual matters may be likened to the seed planted in the womb. If the seed is not kept there, secret and sacred, and fed from within, it never will become being. Secrecy is the womb of the spiritual life, and every experience should be taken right into that womb and kept sacred.

"I", Crying out

The ancient Hebrew prophets were looked upon as something set apart and great because they could prophesy. The truth is that there was nothing unusual about this at all. You will find that the two things they prophesied were that those who were living in bondage to limitation and holding others in that same limitation were going to be destroyed, and that those who were seeking freedom were going to attain it. That is what they prophesied: the doom of those who were kings, those who were tyrants, those who were limited.

It is just as easy to prophesy such things today because as you unfold spiritually you will come to realize that the only permanent thing in the world is whatever conforms to a law of God. This is the only thing that eventually is going to be the permanent status of man. Therefore, you can prophesy that any teaching of a way of life that takes away from man his freedom and his individuality is doomed. In all current totalitarian ideologies, man is considered to be a part of a mass, a part of a herd. That cannot continue or last because the *I* is crying out for escape.

Not only did the Hebrews cry out for freedom from Pharaoh, but the Russians under the Czars cried out for freedom; the English cried out for freedom until they wrested first the Magna Carta and later the Bill of Rights from their rulers. The French cried out for freedom until an aroused populace brought to an end the tyrannical rule that had held them in bondage.

Today man is crying inside himself for freedom because man is not man: man is God individualized, and God is not going to stay locked up in man forever, nor is God going to stay locked up in a trade union that tells anyone how much he can earn and when he can or cannot earn it, or in a country that dictates where and how he must live, or in any other form of suppression. No! All these things are doomed. Anything that restricts or limits is doomed because God is the mind of man, and that mind will not forever be limited or restricted or held in bondage. Do not ever think that it will. It *will* break through!

For thousands of years, education was denied to all but the few. Today, however, literacy programs are being introduced into the most remote and backward areas of the world, awakening man to his potentialities. This, in itself, is an indication of a major breakthrough in setting man free. You cannot continue to hold an educated man in bondage. The moment he begins to learn and to know, he begins to *be,* and you cannot hold him in slavery any longer.

Because the *I* of man is God, begin right now to be a prophet and prophesy that the ultimate destiny of man is freedom. He does not have to bring it about by wars; he does not have to bring it about by rebellion. "Be still, and know that I am God." Sit still, and know that *I* am God, and soon those out in the world will begin setting you free, and they will not know why.

Yes, you can prophesy that the destiny of this world is freedom from sin, disease, death, from bondage, and from limitation. The beginning of that freedom comes with the realization of the nature of *I.* That is enough! That one truth will begin to break all the crusts of limitation and outside powers that bind you. Just be still.

"Be still, and know that I *am God. . . .* I *will never leave thee."* I *am thy bread;* I *am thy intelligence;* I *am thy safety;* I *am thy security.*

In that stillness, you have gone beyond words and thoughts to the very Center of all being, and there you can rest.

SCRIPTURAL REFERENCES
AND NOTES

The material in *Beyond Words and Thoughts* has been taken from tape-recorded lectures and classes given by Joel S. Goldsmith in 1963. It first appeared in print in the form of monthly letters sent to students of the Infinite Way throughout the world as an aid to the revelation and unfoldment of the transcendental consciousness through a deeper understanding of Scripture and the principles of the Infinite Way.

Chapter 1
1. John 18:36
2. Isaiah 2:22
3. I Samuel 3:9
4. I Corinthians 15:31
5. John 17:3
6. Proverbs 3:6
7. II Corinthians 3:6
8. *The Cloud of Unknowing,* Trans. by Ira Progoff. (New York: The Julian Press, 1957).
9. I Corinthians 2:14
10. Romans 8:7
11. Luke 12:40
12. Luke 22:42
13. Matthew 18:12, 13
14. Ephesians 4:22, 24
15. II Chronicles 32:8
16. Matthew 5:39

Chapter 2
1. John 18:36
2. Matthew 5:39

Chapter 2 (Continued)
3. Matthew 26:52
4. Psalm 16:11
5. Mark 6:50
6. Galatians 2:20
7. Revelation 21:27
8. Ephesians 4:22
9. Matthew 19:17
10. Matthew 23:27
11. Isaiah 2:22
12. Galatians 6:8
13. Stephen Decatur
14. John 10:30
15. John 16:33
16. Romans 6:16
17. Matthew 6:25
18. Luke 12:40
19. John 14:6

Chapter 3
1. Galatians 2:20
2. Psalm 46:1
3. Psalm 91:10
4. Psalm 91:1

Chapter 3 (Continued)
5. John 5:14
6. Luke 7:48
7. Daniel 3:27
8. Luke 15:31
9. Matthew 17:5
10. II Corinthians 12:9
11. Alfred, Lord Tennyson, *The Higher Pantheism*, Stanza 6
12. Isaiah 2:22
13. John 5:31
14. Matthew 13:46
15. John 12:45
16. Isaiah 26:3
17. Proverbs 3:5, 6

Chapter 4
1. *A Parenthesis in Eternity*, by the author
2. Lectures and classes given by Mr. Goldsmith during 1963 were tape-recorded and are available to students.
3. *The Infinite Way,* by the author
4. John 14:6
5. John 5:30, 31
6. John 12:45
7. John 10:17
8. Matthew 4:4
9. Isaiah 45:2
10. Matthew 6:25
11. John 4:31, 32
12. John 7:16
13. John 16:7
14. Exodus 3:14
15. Hebrews 4:12

Chapter 5
1. Luke 22:35
2. Luke 12:31
3. I Corinthians 3:16
4. I Corinthians 6:19
5. Isaiah 2:22
6. Matthew 5:48
7. I Corinthians 2:14
8. John 14:27
9. John 14:10
10. Philippians 4:13
11. Matthew 7:14
12. John 6:26
13. John 6:68
14. Matthew 4:20
15. Luke 14:15-24
16. Isaiah 65:24
17. Genesis 18:32
18. Romans 8:26
19. Matthew 4:4
20. Philippians 2:5
21. John 12:32

Chapter 6
1. John 9:25
2. Ephesians 4:22
3. Ephesians 4:24
4. Matthew 21:12
5. Philippians 3:13, 14
6. Luke 23:34
7. Matthew 4:20
8. Matthew 6:19, 20
9. I Corinthians 15:26
10. I Samuel 3:9
11. Galatians 2:20
12. Luke 21:33
13. Matthew 25:45

Chapter 7
1. Galatians 2:20

Chapter 7 (Continued)
2. John 5:30
3. John 14:10
4. II Chronicles 32:8
5. Genesis 18:32
6. Zechariah 4:6
7. Matthew 25:40
8. Matthew 25:45

Chapter 8
1. Matthew 4:4
2. Corinthians 3:17
3. II Corinthians 12:9
4. Luke 22:42
5. Alfred, Lord Tennyson, *The Higher Pantheism,* Stanza 6
6. John 8:58
7. Robert Browning
8. John 12:45
9. John 10:30
10. Zechariah 4:6

Chapter 9
1. Matthew 19:17
2. John 18:36

Chapter 10
1. Matthew 6:25, 33
2. Moses Maimonides. *The Guide of the Perplexed.* Translated with an introduction and notes by Schlom Pines. (Chicago, Illinois: University of Chicago Press, 1963). Pp. xxi-xxvii.
3. This book was given to Joel Goldsmith by a

Chapter 10 (Continued)
student early in September, 1963.
4. Hebrews 13:5
5. Isaiah 43:5
6. John 10:30
7. Galatians 3:28
8. Luke 15:31
9. Psalm 24:1
10. Isaiah 2:22
11. Galatians 3:28

Chapter 11
1. I Samuel 3:9
2. By the author
3. Galatians 6:8
4. John 6:35
5. John 11:25
6. John 4:14
7. Isaiah 45:2
8. John 14:2
9. Isaiah 2:22
10. Isaiah 1:18
11. John 18:36
12. Matthew 5:39
13. Matthew 19:19
14. Deuteronomy 6:4

Chapter 12
1. Exodus 3:14
2. John 10:30
3. Luke 17:20, 21
4. Luke 15:31
5. John 4:32
6. Matthew 14:27
7. Hebrews 13:5
8. By the author
9. John 12:45
10. John 9:25
11. Luke 4:8

Scriptural References and Notes

Chapter 12 (Continued)
12. John 14:6
13. John 5:31
14. John 8:58
15. Luke 17:21

Chapter 12 (Continued)
16. John 14:27
17. Isaiah 2:22
18. I Corinthians 2:14
19. Psalm 46:10